INSIDE LEFT

DEREK HATTON

INSIDE LEFT

THE STORY SO FAR ...

BLOOMSBURY

First published 1988

Copyright © 1988 by Mercury Press Agency Limited
Bloomsbury Publishing Limited, 2 Soho Square, London W1V 5DE

British Library Cataloguing in Publication Data
Hatton, Derek
Inside left: the story so far.
1. (Metropolitan county). Merseyside.
Liverpool. Politics. Hatton, Derek.
Biographies
I. Title
942.7′53′.0924

ISBN 0 7475 0185 8

Designed by The Fish Family
Phototypeset by Falcon Graphic Art Ltd
Wallington, Surrey
Printed in Great Britain by
Richard Clay Ltd, Bungay, Suffolk

TO SHIRL, BECKY, BEN, SARAH AND LAURA,
MAM, DAD – THE FORTY-NINE AND THE
PEOPLE OF LIVERPOOL

CONTENTS

	Acknowledgements	ix
	Prologue	xiii
ONE	The Wrong Side of the Tracks	1
TWO	Starting Out	12
THREE	Inside Militant	24
FOUR	The Battle for Croxteth	45
FIVE	Days of Revolution	56
SIX	Liverpool versus London	73
SEVEN	The Net Closes	86
EIGHT	The Enemy Within	98
NINE	Muck Raking	111
TEN	True Blue Hatton	130
ELEVEN	The Witch-Hunt	138
TWELVE	The Final Hours	154
	Epilogue	167

ACKNOWLEDGEMENTS

During my three and a half years as deputy leader of Liverpool City Council, and in the past 15 years in the city, there were so many people who helped and supported me, both in my political activities and in my personal life. Many of them were instrumental in helping put together this record of that period of my life, and I would like gratefully to acknowledge their help and pass on my special thanks to others. They come not in order of significance, but simply in alphabetical order.

There were of course "the forty-nine", the Labour councillors of Liverpool who were the most loyal group you could ever find: Heather Adams, Paul Astbury, Michael Black, Dominic Brady, Edward Burke, Tony Byrne, Jacqueline Crowley, Hugh Dalton, Joseph Devaney, James Dillon, Alex Doswell, Felicity Dowling, Pauline Dunlop, Stephen Ellison, Peter Ferguson, Alan Fogg, Alex Gamble, Roy Gladden, Jimmy Hackett, John Hamilton, William Harper, Tony

Hood, John Humphries, Stephen Jenkins, Paul Lafferty, Bill Lafferty, Robert Lancaster, David Leach, John Linden, David Lloyd, George Lloyd, Peter Lloyd, Paul Luckock, John McIntosh, Dorothy Mathews, Francis Mills, Tony Mulhearn, John Nelson, John Ord, Peter Owens, James Parry, Terence Prout, Tony Rimmer, James Rutledge, Henry Smith, Vincent Wagner, Billestbury, Francis Wiles.

My thanks also go to the following: Lynn Anderson, Roger Bannister, Tony Beyga, Sandra Bowman, Keva Coombes, Dave Cotterill, Collette D'Arcy, David Davies, Peter Dougherty, Everton Football Club, Terry Fields, Ian Harris, Eric Heffer, Rowena Jones, Johnny Kennedy, George Knibb, Eddie Loyden, Pat McIlhinney, Denise Myerson, Andy Pink, Ronnie Stephenson, Alfred Stocks, Peter Taaffe, Cathy Toner, Jim Tonner, The Vernon Arms, Dave Ware, Jimmy Wilson, Woolton Labour Club, Bob Wylie, and all those others who in the past 15 years made their individual contributions and assisted me in so many ways.

Last, but not least, my editor, Roger Blyth, for his skill and untiring patience. Without him this book would never have been started, let alone finished.

Editor's Note:

Apart from those people whose role has already been acknowledged by Derek, some of whom helped me in the often complex task of piecing together his story, there are those whose assistance I personally would like to acknowledge.

Derek himself of course – or "Degsy" as we in Liverpool know him – and his wife Shirley. My research assistant Kieron Collins, for his delving and digging, and non-stop flow of caffeine and good humour. My thanks also go to those who helped prepare the manuscript and material which went into it: Alec Copeland, Vic Gibson, Christine Halls, Steve Hanson, Wendy Heap, Pat Peter, Ann Fillis and Laura Walsh.

I gratefully acknowledge the following organisations and photographers for the use of their material in this book: Mercury Press Agency Ltd (Neil Jones, Tony Hall, David

Boyle, Jimmy Clarke), the Liverpool Daily Post and Echo Ltd, the *St Helens Reporter*. Derek and I would like to express our appreciation of the help and insight given by Kathy Rooney, Sian Facer and all at Bloomsbury Publishing.

Finally my personal thanks to my co-director Rose Kirkby, Sian Bradshaw and the staff at Mercury for their support and encouragement, and to Karen Dawkins, for her patience, loyalty and guidance – and for keeping my nose to the grindstone.

R.P.B. December 1987

PROLOGUE

The last thing Karl Marx said before he died in 1883 was: "Last words are for fools who haven't said enough." So this is not my political obituary.

True, no one could live through the past three and a half years as I have done, without a feeling of sadness that it has all come to an end. But while there are a million more things for Derek Hatton to do, those three and a half years will never be wiped out. Neither will they be forgotten in the political history books. If I do nothing else now in my life, I will have done more than most people have with theirs.

Those are not the boasts of someone they've called "The Mouth". They are a fact of life. They can exile me to the political wilderness, they can say that they finally beat me but when the history books are written for the 1980s the names of Militant and Derek Hatton will be right there, alongside those of Kinnock and Thatcher, as a reminder that the working classes can and will win. That victory is inevitable.

One of the things that worried the establishment and the Tory party in particular was not the fact that I was a Labour politician, or that I ran Liverpool City Council. It was the fact that we actually made commitments, and kept our promises.

We were not the loony left – more concerned about black mayors and gay rights than we were about building new homes. We said we would build houses, and we did; five thousand homes were built in three and a half years, more than twice the number of every other city in the country put together. We told the establishment, "Irrespective of what you say, irrespective of what you think, irrespective of whether you give us the money or not, we are going to go out and do this." The people of Liverpool supported us. That is what worried Thatcher. That is what still worries Kinnock.

On the day that I resigned as deputy leader of the council, as I walked out of the municipal buildings in the city centre, a woman of about fifty came running up to me, crying her eyes out, and said, "What have those bastards done to you? They have no right. It's not their city. It's ours."

A few minutes later, as I was crossing the road to go for a drink in the Vernon Arms across from my office a car pulled up alongside me and four young Scousers who had just heard the headlines on the lunchtime news shouted out: "You stay in there. Don't let them grind you down – you'll do for us."

It's that strength of feeling which those who have opposed me, and those who have opposed Militant in Liverpool, have underestimated and misjudged.

They may have thrown me out, but if they think Militant is defeated they have seriously miscalculated. Like it or not, Neil Kinnock has Militant fighting on his side. He called us maggots, gnawing at the core of the Labour Party. He will discover that we are the core.

O N E

THE WRONG SIDE OF THE TRACKS

People have often accused me of being a show-off, a showman, someone who loves hogging the limelight. I suppose there's a degree of truth in it too.

The irony is, going back to my schooldays, that if I'd had my way I would have been an actor. I was even given the chance of touring Germany with the National Youth Theatre. That only happened because I loathed and detested school, and ended up in a production of *The Merchant of Venice* as a way of skipping lessons.

You only have to read my school reports to see what the teachers made of Derek Hatton. In 1959, at the age of eleven, I had passed the eleven-plus, and to the delight of Mam and Dad their only son won himself a place at the prestigious Liverpool Institute.

But by the end of the summer term, in July 1960, twelve-year-old Derek Hatton was third from the bottom of class 3D, and headmaster J. R. Edwards was warning: "His position is disgraceful, and his place in the school is in jeopardy." I obviously took very little notice, because six months later, by the Christmas of 1960, Mr Edwards wrote on my school report: "Next term will decide whether he stays in this school," while my maths teacher observed that I wasted time by talking! I wonder what he would make of the amount of talking I've done since those days!

My mother was constantly being called to the school to be told what a disgrace I was, but in spite of all the threats to expel me, I somehow managed to stay on till I was sixteen, largely, I suspect, due to the fear of what repercussions there would have been at home had the Institute thrown me out.

The eleven-plus in those days was important. If you passed you were going on to grammar school, and when you left, the chances were you would be well placed for a professional career.

My mother was so proud that I had made it through the exams, and won a place at the Institute, which was a massive school, with six forms of entry, and around forty pupils to each class. As far as she was concerned I was there – and I was there to stay. As those school reports showed, though, I didn't particularly like school. From the moment I got there I lived for playing football and cricket. That's all I did. So the next year I was moved into the E stream, and for the rest of my time there I fluctuated between the E and F streams.

With hindsight, and against a background of huge national debates over education, it's interesting to reflect that you had a situation in those days where all the teachers who taught the higher streams had degrees. The majority teaching the lower classes did not. So the pupils in the top three streams were destined for university, those in the D stream and below were looking towards technical college. The rest of us down at the bottom of the grades were the also-rans, merely there on sufferance.

I had no inclination at the time to go through exams and schooling. I didn't want to know. I was far more interested

2

in football. So from then on, because they showed no interest in me, I wasn't interested in them. I was good at football, and started playing more and more. It has been an abiding passion ever since. As I grew older the sportsmasters like Nobby Clarke and Algie Goodall, who, it has to be said, gave me tremendous encouragement on the sportsfield used to let me help coach some of the younger pupils who were coming in to the first year. They even gave me time off lessons to do it. So when I should have been studying I was on the soccer field.

I became more and more entrenched in my attitude that I didn't want to know about learning. I found no encouragement off the soccer field, and the school and I developed a strange relationship. In one way I hated it. In other respects I tolerated it.

That was the way things remained until the last year. Then, one morning, as we were in the hall for assembly, there was an announcement that there was to be a school play. One of my pals said: "We'll have a go at that." I said "You must be joking." He said "Yes, what you do is you apply for a part, but don't get it, so then they ask you to do the props. That way you get all sorts of time off classes." I thought "Time off for football, time off for the play. I'll never be in class. This is great."

So off we went to audition for *The Merchant of Venice*. What we didn't anticipate was that I landed a part – but I was chosen to play Gratiano. That had never been any part of the plan. The last thing I had seen myself doing was dressing up in costume and standing on the stage. But as things turned out I loved it and what's more I was good at it. If someone had said to me, "You should go in the school play," I would have laughed my head off. Now, for the first time in all those years at the Institute, I found myself involved in something other than football which I liked. More than that, for the first time someone really believed in me.

They had never done that before. Just think of the thousands and thousands of talented kids who go through the school system but get no encouragement or acknowledgement – the system which said that unless you could demonstrate

3

academic talents you were finished for life. If you failed the eleven-plus you were pushed into a secondary modern, and left to find your own salvation. That perhaps says more about my absolute conviction that comprehensive schools are the only way forward for the education system than anything else.

The big break which could have taken me into the acting profession came on the last night of *The Merchant of Venice*. Billy Kenwright, who went on to star in *Coronation Street* and is now a London impresario with a fine string of productions behind him, was playing the part of Shylock. I was so keen that not only had I learned the part of Gratiano, but I was understudying Billy as well, and we struck up quite a friendship. On the last evening one of his friends, who was a director with the National Youth Theatre, came backstage at the end, and asked how I would like to join them on a summer tour of Germany.

I was desperate to go. That week on stage had me burning with the realisation that this was something I could do, something I was good at.

It's strange really because I don't have a particularly good memory. I can't learn things. I hear songs a few times, but don't remember the lines. On stage it was different. I wanted to succeed, and concentrated my entire mind on it.

I remember every night of that production vividly. I was a part of it. There was a collective responsibility. We all desperately wanted it to go right. It was like playing football. We all wanted to win. Not only that, but as an individual it was the first time I had been in the limelight, and I loved every minute of it. Mind you Dad always says to me: "I wasn't surprised about that. Whenever you used to play football, whenever you made a good tackle, whenever you scored, you always used to look around to see who was applauding."

I don't think Mam and Dad missed a single night of the school production. They loved the idea of my being up there at the front of stage, and imagine how my life might have changed if I had taken the opportunity to go on into an acting career.

4

But it was my mother, always an enormous influence on me, who put paid to any ideas I had of going off to the world of theatre. She was having none of it. She had arranged for me to start an apprenticeship at Plesseys Electrical Engineering works in Liverpool, and left me in no doubt that was where my future lay. "You've got an apprenticeship and the chance of a good job," she told me. "You should think yourself damned lucky."

Alma Hatton may only be a little woman physically, but like many Liverpool mothers before her she ruled our home and our lives with a rod of iron, tempered with genuine concern and compassion. But God help you if you put a foot wrong – and I frequently did. My father, George, a fireman for twenty-eight years until 1974, and a fine strong figure of a man, has never laid a hand on me in his life. To this day I have always had immense respect and love for him. But if I had a pound for every time Mam has given me a clip round the ear I could buy two more of those expensive suits that everyone spends so much time talking about.

Mam and Dad still live to this day in the council semi in Childwall Valley, Liverpool, where I grew up from the age of two. Until that time, they had lived in rented rooms in Liverpool. That was where I was born on January 17th, 1948. Unusually for a Liverpool family, I was an only child, but like every Liverpool kid I was also part of a huge extended family of cousins, aunties and uncles.

There was always the big family house in Wavertree, Liverpool, only a mile and a half outside the city centre, where my Grandfather lived and Grandmother. She was the centre of it all. At Christmas, on New Year's Eve and on any special occasion, the whole family would congregate there. It was one of those big old houses built in the days of large families in a city, where with its strong Irish-Catholic history big families weren't the exception but the norm. Even on the other side of the sectarian fence – the whole of my family has a Protestant background – big families were quite standard, and matriarchs like Gran ruled the roost. On high days and holidays we kids went in one room, and parents in another. But before ever you went into one room with the rest of the kids you had to go into the back and say "Hello" to Grandmother first. She would then give you permission to go into the other room. It was that sort of discipline. She sat there on her chair by the fire and controlled everyone, including Grandad.

He was a muscular man with immense strength, and worked as a blacksmith. Every day he walked the twelve miles to work in neighbouring Formby, and then walked back, just to save money. He would set out at six in the morning and get back at eight at night. Then when the bronchitis which eventually killed him became too much, he had to retire, and became a school crossing patrol warden.

In family terms though it was Grandma who was the strength, and it's exactly the same with my mother now. Mam is five foot nothing but a very very powerful little individual. She controls everything, the house, the money, and Dad, even though he is a powerfully built six-foot ex-Coldstream Guards boxing champion and an ex-English Schoolboys footballer.

My mother's family were a quieter crowd. There was Nan and Pop along with Great Auntie Ivy and Uncle Tony. He was a draughtsman at Plesseys all his life, and an aircraft fitter during the war. Though he has a very practical side to his nature – he was always the one you would find under a car fixing it – he also has a very lively, enquiring mind. It was Tony who early in my life taught me to question people's views and opinions, and to take nothing for granted.

In many ways I suppose he planted the first thoughts in my head about politics. He has never married to this day, and perhaps because he was a single man, with no children of his own, he saw me as the son he never had. He is an old-school Labour supporter through and through but with a libertarian approach. He always encouraged me to look behind the headlines, and as far as he was concerned, and it's something I probably first picked up from him, politics was about people. I remember him saying that when I was old enough I shouldn't take voting for granted. According to him it was no good

6

moaning about the state of the world if you didn't do something about it yourself.

His kindness to me was considerable. So was his influence, and both have been transferred to my own children.

We lived in Childwall Valley Road, on the east side of the city, in an area which undoubtedly influenced the way I later came to think and feel about society. The thing which always struck me about it was that it was just like the saying which originated in Chicago in the 1920s that some people were born "on the wrong side of the track". We lived alongside an old disused railway track which runs from Bowring Park Road right through to Woolton, in the posh south residential end of Liverpool. Every house to one side of the track was private. To the other side, where we lived, every home was a "corpy" (corporation) house. So it was just us and the prefabs – and the nobs who lived up the hill.

They had the church, they had the youth club, and because there was nowhere else to go and nothing else to do, my pals and I would end up going there and mixing with them. Even at that very early stage I remember feeling almost as though I was from a different camp, a different world.

I either went up the hill to All Saints Church in Childwall where I went to youth club – and believe it or not even sang in the choir – or I went to the back field to play football. I still have the photographs of me as a choir boy to remind me of that period.

When I wasn't doing that I would jump on one of the old green trams, and go down to the waterfront where Dad was based for years with the Fire Brigade in Colberg and Canada Docks and at Fire Brigade headquarters, which ironically are based of all places in Hatton Garden!

Those were the days when Liverpool boasted an overhead railway which ran the length of the docks on the banks of the Mersey. It was nicknamed the "Dockers' Umbrella" and as a kid I would take the overhead down to the fire station just to spend time looking at the engines and listening to Dad and his

7

mates swapping stories. He often came home smelling of smoke if he had been out on a big job, and would tell me tales of the jobs he had been out on.

One of the earliest recollections I have where Dad is concerned is him telling me how he and three other firemen had been trapped on the top floor of a blazing building during a huge rubber fire down on the docks. They only escaped by sliding down the hose pipe which they had taken up to the top of the blazing building with them. On another occasion he remembers me rushing home from school, very proudly, having seen his picture along with that of his crew, in the *Liverpool Echo*, after a fire in which they had tried to save the lives of two elderly people trapped in a blazing house.

There were many times when he came home quite exhausted and drained by it all, especially in the fires where people had lost their lives like the huge blaze at Henderson's, a city centre store in Liverpool, where eleven people died in 1960.

He has been a huge influence in my life, and so, in spite of all its unpleasant moments, was the job he did. So much so that later I was to go on and join the Fire Service myself.

But from the age of fourteen onwards one of the most important things in my life was the part-time job I landed at Jackson's the Tailors, helping out in their store in Church Street, in the centre of the city, on Saturdays and during the school holidays.

If anyone asks where I got my taste for dressing well, I suppose it was there. Dad had always been an immaculate dresser, and I couldn't resist good clothes even then, so I would put down a deposit on a suit costing £20 or £30 and tell Mam that the price of the deposit was the price of the suit. She would have gone wild had she known the truth. In fact to this day I've never told her.

I remember clearly I used to get fifteen shillings for working a Saturday. Fourpence was taken out for a stamp, and my mother took four shillings and eightpence out of it, leaving me

8

ten bob. She always used to say: "It's not because I need it, but because it's good for you."

Working in the tailor's shop, helping measure up for suits, and tidying the stock, was good for me in terms of discipline and responsibility. From that day to this hard work has never frightened me. I loved getting up early to go in, and I could go on working till the clock went round. It was a habit which stood me in good stead when I moved into politics.

I even kept the job on when at sixteen I started my apprenticeship. That was almost as big a disaster as school had been. I was training as a technician on telephone installations, but it just wasn't me. I was bored out of my mind, and before long Mam and Dad were being called in to Plesseys, just as they had been at school, to be told: "If your Derek doesn't improve then he'll have to go." The job lasted just six months until the early part of 1965.

It ended with Mam in tears, and me going off to work as an office clerk in the Royal Liver Friendly Society, at their offices at Liverpool's Pier Head – the Liver Building, which, with its twin towers and mythical Liver Birds on top, is probably the one image of the city which always stays in everyone's minds. I stayed there until 1966, but it was a nine-till-five job which was never the sort of career for which I was cut out.

I was working in the treasurer's department, pushing paper across desks all day long and working on claims forms. But even though the job itself didn't suit me, I still had my weekend job at the tailor's store, and at least my office job opened up the whole of my social life.

I might not have landed a place centre-stage in the theatre, but I soon found my niche as leader of the pack with a whole gang of lads from the office who knocked around together after work and on Saturday nights. Liverpool in those days, in the 1960s really was the centre of the music world. The Beatles were at their height, and the Cavern Club was in full swing.

I had in fact been at school with two of the Beatles, Paul McCartney and George Harrison. Paul is older than me, and was in his last year when I first started at the Institute. But I

9

remember as though it was yesterday sharing detention with him one night. I had been given an hour's detention, by the art master Stan Reed. I hated art, and found myself having to stay on after school in the Art Room to finish work I hadn't done during class.

But Paul McCartney loved art, and was there of his own accord, doing extra work just for the fun of it. Even then he was involved with local bands, and we spent the whole hour talking about pop groups and music. He was a bit of a hero to all the lads in school because he and the Beatles had already begun playing in the evenings and at weekends down at the Cavern Club in Matthew Street in the centre of Liverpool, and at local youth clubs.

I can't honestly say I remember that much about George Harrison, who was several years older than me, and a much quieter character than McCartney ever was.

Every Tuesday and Friday night we would go out to the Mardi Gras, a dance hall club up the hill out of the city centre in Mount Pleasant to listen to groups like The Escorts and Cy Tucker and The Friars. The Victoriana, another night-club down by the old Mersey Tunnel entrance, was another of our haunts. And of course there was the Cavern itself, in Matthew Street. Today the original Cavern is buried under the rubble where a new shopping precinct, Cavern Walks, has been built – though for all that it's still Mecca for Beatles fans from all over the world. But at that time John Lennon, Paul McCartney and the rest had become world famous, and the Cavern was home to every band who wanted to make it through to the big time.

Looking back it seems as though we spent almost every night out on the town night-clubbing and chatting up the girls. When we weren't in the clubs we were at all-night parties, taking our first taste of booze and tobacco and generally behaving like the rest of teenage Britain in a city which almost gave the Swinging Sixties their name.

Strangely though, it was in that twelve months working as an office boy that it first began to occur to me that there was something more important to life. I couldn't identify what I was searching for. I even looked for it in the Church and failed to find it there. Tell anyone now that Derek Hatton was seriously involved with religion, and thought that the Church might provide the answer to life's problems, and they will laugh at you.

The man who influenced me, during that period in 1965, was a curate called Dennis Naden. I still occasionally see him. In his own way he was quite a radical, and after church and youth club, he would organise discussion groups, at which, as teen-agers, we would sit down and try to put the world to rights.

We talked about youth work, about community action, about housing conditions. It wasn't religion in terms of being moralistic. I still went out to the clubs, I still went out with the gangs of lads, I still went out with women. But I felt there was something wrong, and that through youth and community work I could do something about it. Dennis Naden was a great influence. I finally decided, and I still believe it now, that the Church had no answers.

T W O

STARTING OUT

After twelve months as an office boy, I finally decided, in March 1966, to follow my father into the fire service, a four-and-a-half-year period of my life which brought my first involvement with trade unions, and the first stirrings of what I now realise was a political conscience about the way in which people lived.

Dad always says that because he had a reputation as one of the smartest officers in the brigade, I felt I had to live up to his image, and I suppose that's true. I also wanted to live up to his reputation as a fireman.

Those years in the fire service were tremendously rewarding. The training was tough and so were the men with whom you worked. They had to be. You had to work as a disciplined team. You might be sitting in the canteen one minute, arguing blue murder with your opposite number, and five minutes later you could be out on the streets and relying on him to save your life. It taught me a valuable lesson: that you could have your battles with people, and be aggressive, but later you could always work together. It's a lesson I carried into politics with me.

Mind you the fact that my father was in the brigade meant I was given no quarter. I well remember as a skinny little seventeen year old, doing my first training stint, running down the course carrying a ten-stone dummy on my back. I was gasping for breath by the time I'd done it, but when I got there a sub-officer called Tommy Hughes screamed at me: "Just because your old man is George Hatton you can run all the way back again." I was absolutely shattered and spent the next day in bed recovering.

It was not the only time, as Dad will always remind me, that the job proved exhausting. On one night in 1966, soon after joining up, we were called out to a big ship fire in the docks. I was out fighting the fire solidly for five or six hours with the rest of the lads, and in the early hours of the morning a relief crew was sent to take over. I was so shattered that on the way back to base in the van I fell asleep on another fireman's shoulder. They didn't stop ribbing me about it for weeks – and neither did Dad!

There were other lessons too, some not so pleasant. I well remember one day we had turned out to Scotland Road, the main road leading out of Liverpool to the North, where an articulated lorry had jack-knifed. The driver had been giving a French student a lift, and she had been thrown out of the cab, and her head went clean under the back wheels. It was an appalling sight. She had quite simply been pulped. Our job was to swill the remains down the gutter, and most of us felt ill just looking at the carnage. I'll never forget one of the lads calmly getting the hose out to swill down the scene, and saying, "Aye, aye – another one joining the brain drain." It sounds dreadfully heartless, but at that stage that man was invaluable. It taught me that sometimes you have to be absolutely ruthless in order to take other people with you.

I've often thought since that on numerous occasions that's the way I've acted politically. I've been prepared to push people on one side and say "Get on with it – I don't care a damn what you think." Almost to go over the top, just to cut through the emotion.

On other occasions too I would experience the way in which people in Liverpool were forced to live. I well remember going out to Toxteth and seeing a whole family having to exist in just one room. No toilet, no bathroom, no fire. The conditions were something I had never before witnessed, and it made me feel there was something dreadfully wrong with a society which forced any family to live like that. The conviction began to grow that there were other ways I could do something to help. I had joined the Fire Brigades Union when I first began my service, but I wasn't an active member. Indeed I wasn't politically active in any real way at that time. But there was just this feeling inside me that I ought to be doing something more positive.

It was at that time, in 1969, that I met up again with eighteen-year-old Shirley Ward, the girl I was to marry a year later. We had first met four years earlier at the All Saints Youth Club when she was fourteen and I was seventeen. We met in the Childwall Abbey pub, over the road from the youth club, where most of the crowd went after meetings or after church.

Shirley came from a very different background, from the other side of the tracks, the well-to-do side of the railway line. She went to an all-girls grammar school run by Anglican nuns and compared with me she was incredibly bright. Hers was a quiet family, and the first couple of times she was introduced to my family I think it came as quite a shock.

I remember to this day her meeting my Aunt Dot, a great big powerful woman, who would take anyone on. It was the day of the mini-skirt, and the first time Dot met her she said: "That skirt's a bit a short, isn't it?" Shirley didn't know where to put herself. She just froze, but Dot came from a family where you spoke your mind no matter what you said. There was a lot of emotion, a lot of feeling, even among the men in the family. We were a very warm, touching kind of family. The fellers would hug and kiss each other just as much as the women.

At the same time we were very aggressive. There would be constant arguments and battles, but we always came out of it loving one another.

I think Shirley had very mixed impressions of me to start with, but she quickly learnt that although we were noisy and aggressive, we were really a lovable bunch with whom you had to stand your ground or come off second best. As she still says to this day it was an education for her.

'Derek's family, and all his aunts and uncles, would argue the toss till the cows came home, but at the end of it all they would kiss and make up. No one was ever allowed to leave the house without doing that. I had come from a much more traditional background, a much smaller family where issues became more personalised, and you tended not to patch things up as quickly or as well as you could.

There was Mum, who came from a tiny farming community in South Wales, Dad, who until he was invalided out of the force at the age of forty was a Liverpool policeman, and sister Pam, who was really responsible for my meeting Derek in the first place.

Pam is three years younger than I am, but as teenagers we were very close, and, because she was much more outgoing than I was, it was Pam who persuaded me to get out and about. I was quite content just sitting in and doing my own thing, but Pam never thought that was enough.

She would spend most evenings and weekends at the local riding school, at the youth club, or at the pub. In fact I can well remember that it was in the pub that I first met Derek on more than a casual basis. I had gone out for the evening with Pam and a friend, when we ran into Derek and a couple of his friends.

I had always thought of him as very smooth. Even then he was a snappy dresser. After a long conversation I realised that it was wrong to judge him in that way. We all went back for coffee, and before you knew it he had asked me to go out with him. I can even remember the date, June 3rd, as it was the night before my sister's birthday. Soon afterwards I went away for a holiday in Clevedon, staying with a girlfriend and working in a children's home as a holiday job. I wrote to him while I was away, and everything blossomed when I came back.

After that we spent time together at the youth club, went out to the pictures together, or even occasionally froze to death at local gymkhanas watching Pam as she took part in horse-riding events. Derek was very much the radical even then. When he decided to set up and run the youth club late in 1966 he received immense help and encouragement from the curate, Dennis Naden, who became a great friend. It was he who really started Derek thinking, and questioning life. He became more aware, and I suppose I did too.

We would often go out to help old people in their homes, and the experience of seeing the conditions in which they lived, as you cleaned the bathroom, the toilet, and stripped wallpaper hanging from the walls of cold, damp flats, was an eye-opener.

I've always said that Derek just swept me off my feet. He did. I was just eighteen, and still at school. He was in the fire service, had a little car of his own and cut quite a figure. He would arrive at the house in his old Ford Popular, and when he walked in it was like a whirlwind. Dad found it very difficult to cope with him in the early stages. I don't think he had ever known anyone like Derek, and found it very hard to relax with him initially. At home it wasn't a case of speaking when we were spoken to, but Dad's own background meant it was almost like that, and he found it hard to be outgoing and express his feelings. The love was there, but he didn't easily show it.

To be faced with someone as outspoken as Derek, never having had to deal with boys in the family at all, was a revelation to him, especially when it was someone so loving and physical – someone who doesn't just say "Hello – how are you?" but who greets you with a bear hug or a cuddle.

In fact I remember the night in 1970 that Derek and I decided to get married, and Dad's reaction to it. The two of us had been going out for exactly a year, when the chance came for Derek to leave the fire service and go off to college in London to take a course in Community and Youth Work at the University of London Goldsmiths' College. We had to decide whether to get married and both go to London, or whether he would go and I would stay.

These days, of course, I doubt that the question of marriage would even arise, but at that time it really was an either-or issue. I know he did propose to me, though I have to say I can't remember exactly what he said! He is so easy-going that I suppose we just sat down and discussed it. His attitude was that if I wanted to get married then it was up to me, and it was what he wanted too. I do remember, though, him saying to my father "Would it be OK if we got married?", and Dad saying to him, "If you buy me a pint in the pub tonight it will be fine." That was his way.

The wedding was on August 29th, 1970 at All Saints in Childwall. We were due to leave very soon afterwards for London. I say that the wedding wasn't outrageous, but it was the sixties, and flower-power was the rage. We sat and hand-wrote the invitations on psychedelic pink, green and orange cards, and when Derek's Mum asked me what dress I was wearing I told her: "I'm not wearing a dress, I'm wearing trousers!" I could almost read her mind: "Here's my only son marrying this nice girl, and she wants to go down the aisle in trousers."

But I did. It was the hippy period – and all that went with it. Pam and I spent a day in London together looking for the right clothes, but we couldn't find anything, and ended up back in Liverpool buying a cream crêpe trouser suit which I still have to this day. There were maroon patent leather shoes to go with it, and navy blue trouser suits for Pam and for Derek's young cousin who was the bridesmaid. Then there was my outfit for the reception – a kaftan! I look at it now and think "Oh my God!", but at the time it was exactly what I wanted. For all that, Mum and Dad never argued the point once. Dad looked at the trouser suit and said "You look lovely," and I thought to myself: "Oh, you liar. . ."

Pam's stray black mongrel, Flash, ended up at the wedding because in some ways he meant more to me than some of the people who were going to be there. So there he sat, resplendent in his white satin ribbon, right alongside Pam in her bridesmaid's outfit. As for Derek, well, you can probably guess. As ever he was wearing an immaculate suit, with a handkerchief tucked in the top pocket. "Mr Cool" as everyone always calls him.

If the wedding was different, so was the honeymoon. Derek's mother and father came too, and not because we planned it that way! We had arranged to borrow my mother's caravan in South Wales for the week, and Derek's uncle lent us his car. At Lake Bala, on the drive down from Liverpool, it broke down, and we had to wait there until his Mum and Dad arrived to take us the rest of the way.

They stayed the night, which, where Derek's father was concerned, meant we were treated to hours of ribald comments and pointed remarks as we lay in our bunks. What a honeymoon! We laugh about it now, and that's just as well. After all, it is true that in later years you can make up for times like that twenty times over. In fact we've spent countless happy holidays down there at the caravan in the years since we got married.

Moving to London was a big step for me. From living in a comfortable home, with always someone there to talk to when you needed them, I found myself packing everything I possessed into a Bedford van, and moving into a single bedroom in someone else's house. Home for the next two years was to be a room with a view of Nunhead Cemetery, and with Derek away at college every day of the week I really had to learn how to make my own life and become my own person.

The couple who owned the house were wonderful, and it was their example in many ways which inspired me to do something positive with my own life. The landlord, an Indonesian, was blind, and his wife, who came from Manchester, was partially sighted. They got on with their lives as though they had no handicap at all, including looking after their three-year-old son and a small baby. Watching them I soon stopped feeling sorry for myself, and as Derek disappeared off into his brand-new world I decided to create one of my own.

Down at the local shopping centre in Peckham Rye I saw an advertisement for an assistant at a small toy shop, and spent six of the happiest months of my life working there, alongside two West Indian girls and a Cockney who became almost family to me. They kept me going, and the job gave me a sense of purpose. In fact it was with very mixed feelings that I eventually left, to take a job as a nurse at a children's day nursery, where I stayed for the rest of the two years.

I believe it's very important that a woman establishes her own role, and her own position. If I had not taken a conscious decision to do that, then I should simply have been dismissed as Derek's wife.

18

Because he was so active, and involved with so many organisations, it was vital for my own self-respect and preservation, that I had something too in my own right.

Because I could stand on my own two feet, I felt able to join him in the projects with which he became involved.

People say to me now: "I don't know how you stand it." I argue that you either get involved or you part company. There is no other way. Derek was all I had, not just the man I loved but also my greatest friend. So I became more involved in his political activities than I ever thought possible, and along the way made many good and lasting friendships.

By the time he went to London Derek was ready for learning. Politics became a passion. He was discovering so many things for the first time, and was surrounded by people who wanted answers to their own questions. Not that in those early days I always found his outspoken attitude easy to handle. I was quite naive, and where my close friends were concerned, I used to worry how they would react to him, and to his particular brand of politics and passion.

I need not have worried. I well remember the woman who ran the day nursery – a lovely Cockney whose husband was a London cabbie – inviting us round for Sunday dinner. They were very warm and caring people, but Derek was so involved in his course, and in his politics, that I knew he would never stop talking about it.

I thought to myself: "Oh God, I work for her and enjoy my job. What if she doesn't approve of what Derek thinks and the things he does?" So I turned to him and said: "Now don't say too much till we get to know them." Imagine my feelings then, when we eventually arrived at Daisy's home, to discover that both she and her husband were Communists, and they were part of a huge East End family of shop stewards, trade unionists, and Labour Party members! Derek was in his element. Once they knew how involved he was in community work and politics they took to him instantly, and it was the start of a very long and close friendship.

Life was quite exhausting in many ways. Derek was deeply involved in the squatting movement, and it wasn't long before I was playing my part too. I would find myself sitting up all night with a family of squatters, waiting for the bailiffs to arrive, and thinking that five months previously I had been in Liverpool living in comfortable middle class surroundings and going out to the riding stables.'

Shirley was right – the move to London opened up a whole new world to me: the world of politics. The course at Goldsmiths' was a very radical one run by a woman called Josephine Klein. There were 400 applications, and just twenty-five places, but it was like the part in the school play. I'd had a taste of it and wanted it. I went in fighting and won.

I had never been outside Liverpool for more than ten days in my whole life before that, and there I was, with Shirley, going down to London to live for the next two years in a one-roomed bedsit in Peckham. Talk about innocents abroad. If you had taken me out into Trafalgar Square and turned me round twice I wouldn't have known where I was. Fortunately the people on the course were very supportive. They were a totally mixed group. At the top end of the scale were armchair socialists with degrees in theology. At the other end were myself and a couple of others who were raw material just waiting to be moulded.

Some were a more obvious influence on me than others. There was for instance Chas Haney, who was a leading figure in the Ford strikes at Dagenham in the late sixties. Then there was a lad called Jim Radford, who was heavily involved with the anti-nuclear lobby and played a leading part in the Committee of 100.

But the greatest influence was what I saw of housing conditions in London and its suburbs. Bear in mind that until that time I had never seen anything of real life outside Merseyside. It was the period when the squatting movement was coming into its own, and Jim Radford became closely involved in the organisation of the housing campaigns. It fascinated me. I couldn't wait to become a part of it.

It made so much sense. Homeless families were simply saying to councils like Lambeth and Southwark: "There are empty houses which we could use. Give them to us, and an association of the homeless will use them to benefit those who

20

need help. It will provide somewhere for people to live, and we will renovate the property, providing an income through rates for the council until it's time for demolition."

In certain areas – notably, and remarkably, in Lewisham, which was Tory controlled – it worked well. Family consciousness was roused, and the properties were improved and cared for. In Southwark, though, where I became chairman of the housing association, there was an old Stalinist-type Labour authority who said quite simply: "If we can't do it, then no one can." As for dealing with a squatters' association, which is basically what we were, they didn't want to know.

Looking back now with my experience as a Liverpool councillor I can perhaps understand it. Had I been a Southwark councillor I would have been appalled at the idea of drawing up agreements with squatters. The difference though, between their view then and mine now, is that I would have wanted to tear down all that old property and put something new in its place.

So we simply moved the families in, and relied on an act dating back to King Richard which forced the council to go to court on every individual case to have squatters evicted. We met in pubs, in back rooms, in people's homes. For the first time I got to know the West Indian community, and loved their way of life, their food and their traditions. Most of them had never organised themselves before, and organisation was something which came naturally to me. I didn't control or dictate, but being in the chairman's seat allowed me to lead the debates and discussions, and to sway the tactics.

My most vivid memory is of the night we took over Southwark Town Hall, the first time that I hit the headlines I suppose you could say, for taking direct illegal action over something I believed in. It was the night of the council's monthly meeting, on April 21st, 1971, and they had refused to meet us and discuss the whole issue of squatting. I discovered that before the meeting, all the councillors got together for a cup of tea in an anteroom, and then arrived in the chamber together.

21

I tipped off the press, then, literally five or ten minutes before the council meeting was due to start, we walked into the chamber, chained the door behind us, and took it over for our own meeting. I sat in the mayor's chair, and eventually they had to come and talk to us. We told them they could have their chamber back if they would sit down and discuss the housing problem.

On May 10th, 1971 we used the same tactics again at Transport House of all places, where we took over one of the offices. Of course it did attract publicity, and though it was gimmicky, I felt satisfied that at least people's political consciousness was being raised, and they felt themselves involved.

To be truthful though it had no long-term effect. As a gesture it was exciting, but what would it finally achieve? Perhaps that's why these days I get angry with people who take direct action against Labour councils, without attacking the situation on the political front as well.

I still can't forgive people who take that sort of action simply to safeguard their own jobs, their own positions, or just to court publicity. I've learned that it gets you nowhere. That was why when I first went back to Liverpool, and took my zeal for housing campaigns with me, we involved Labour councillors from the start, and used political as well as direct action.

By now my two years in London were almost over. Shirley and I had spent almost every weekend chugging up and down the motorway to Merseyside in a battered old blue Volkswagen, and both of us needed to get get back to our roots.

London had certainly changed my perspective, but by then in 1972 I was ready to go back to Liverpool. I had made good friends in London, but some of the people we had met, especially from the college where I had studied, were academics who tended to see life from an armchair. I was used to what I called real people, and back in Liverpool I knew I would find them again. What's more, after all my experiences in London and having become for the first time actively involved with politics I needed something else. I knew it was no good standing on the outside shouting and screaming about the problems of society. The only way to do anything was to get inside and work there.

I was soon to be introduced to a group who thought exactly as I did. Militant.

T H R E E

INSIDE MILITANT

Shirley and I arrived back in Liverpool with two things in mind. We needed somewhere to live – and I needed a job. With the Goldsmiths' Certificate in Community and Youth Work in my pocket I applied for a post as the director of a community scheme which had been set up in Liverpool by, among other people, John Moores Junior, the son of Liverpool football pools millionaire Sir John Moores. It was called the Bronte Centre Neighbourhood Organisation and though it had started out as a boys' club it had developed into a community operation providing facilities for leisure and recreation. By the time I arrived in July 1972 it had become much more concerned with solving housing problems and trying to provide employment opportunities.

This was all at the time when the Conservatives under Ted Heath had introduced their Housing Finance Act. The Labour Party was dead set against it and with the experiences of the battles on the housing front in Southwark behind me I soon became involved myself. It was the Act which had triggered off a whole series of rent strikes on Merseyside and elsewhere, because it led to council house rents being raised all over the country. The fear was too that ultimately it would have the effect of taking control of council house rent structures away from the local authorities. It was ultimately to be repealed in 1974 when Labour came to power under Harold Wilson.

The Bronte Centre was, from my point of view, a natural home for this kind of revolt. It's a large brick building just outside the city centre, set up as a charitable trust in the days when community centres were a fairly new concept. Pensioners' parties, kids' outings and of course bingo were all part and parcel of the day-to-day routine there and it was my job to oversee all those activities. The original boys' club was an old paint warehouse in Bronte Street, but in 1973 the Centre moved to its new headquarters in neighbouring Trowbridge Street. Now it became an umbrella organisation which ran everything from boxing tournaments for youngsters to a community centre for the elderly.

But the Bronte serves one of the most deprived working-class areas of Liverpool. Nearby is the Bullring, one of those vast soul-destroying complexes of flats built before the Second World War. Housing conditions there were absolutely appalling, yet the then Labour Council in Liverpool seemed to do nothing about them, and the tenants there – many of them the very people who used the Bronte Centre – had no one to lead the fight against authority.

It was a soapbox tailor-made for Derek Hatton at a time when I really wanted to get actively involved in changing the conditions I saw all around me in Liverpool.

That, I suppose, was where I began to run into trouble at the Bronte Centre. Initially John Moores Junior and I got on well. In the early days, I would even visit his home to have discussions with him and his wife Jane. He could be very critical of the Tory Government, and constantly argued for change. I think he honestly believed it, but whether with his background it was really possible for him to be a part of that change is another matter.

Before long we were at loggerheads. I wanted to see the money from the Bronte Centre diverted into housing campaigns and used to help the fight for better conditions for the people who lived around it. The Bronte Council, of which he was the chairman, saw it, in my view, as a business and wanted the profits to be ploughed back in.

For two years we battled it out and without any doubt I was rapidly becoming an embarrassment to the Bronte – because now I had become a political animal. I freely admit on reflection that the job I was supposed to do began to suffer. Managing the Centre began to take second place as I became more and more involved with the fight against the local authority. I was coming to realise that the only solution to Liverpool's problems was a political solution. Maybe if the Bronte Centre had simply employed me as a community worker and not as the director things would have worked out. As it was, by 1974 I decided to quit.

During the whole of those two years Shirley and I were living in a little terraced house we had found off Smithdown Road just outside the city. Shirley had spent the first year at night classes to pick up some formal qualifications as a nursery nurse. Then she took a job as a social-work assistant out in Netherley, a huge council estate on the outskirts of Liverpool where she spent her time helping pensioners and handicapped children. In her spare time she helped me during the evenings and weekends at the Bronte Centre and she was always conscious of the gap which existed between the lives of the people she met there and the lives of others.

On the one hand she would visit a single mother struggling to make ends meet in appalling housing conditions in the Bullring only to find herself offered hospitality which would be overwhelming. People there didn't have twopence to spare, but would sacrifice the tinned ham, cakes and any other little luxuries they had stored away just to make you feel welcome and needed.

On the other hand at the Bronte Centre helpers like Shirley would be invited to a "treat" by the management committee, only to find that it was a very ordinary "bunfight", the sort of spread Shirley would lay on any teatime at home. To this day she still remembers one girl pointing at the table and saying: "Oh God – look at the caviar." It was brown pickle!

It was in 1974 just before I left my job in the Bronte Centre that I first became involved with the Labour Party. I had always known that Socialism was correct but I didn't want to know about fringe organisations like the Communist Party or the Socialist Workers' Party. As far as I was concerned they were Mickey Mouse outfits. At the same time I didn't know whether I could exist within the Labour Party itself. It was ultimately the influence of a Liverpool Labour councillor, Dr Cyril Taylor, that led me to join. In the early 1970s he was regarded as a radical figure in Liverpool and we met during my time at the Bronte while I was planning the launch of a local community newspaper.

We talked and talked, though I guess as usual I did most of the talking. I remember him asking me "Why the hell aren't you in the Labour Party?" He pushed and pushed until I joined the constituency party in the Edge Hill ward. To this day I remember that I went round canvassing for the local MP, Sir Arthur Irvine, a man whose view of Socialism I despised. I recollect thinking to myself, as he walked round waving his brolly and with his big hanky stuffed in his top pocket, "Christ Almighty, what am I doing with this fella?" I felt positively embarrassed going into pubs with him.

But I was still fired with political ambition and wanted to get out there and do something. My chance came in the summer of 1974. On January 25th, 1974 Rebecca, the first of our four children, had been born at the Oxford Street Maternity Hospital in Liverpool. She was a beautiful child, in fact I used to describe her as "the baby with the kissable lips". But on the very day that Shirley came home from hospital with her I was being interviewed by a journalist from a local paper after all the uproar about my political activities at the Bronte Centre.

And by July that year, with Becky only six months old, I had given up my job and was travelling twice a week to Sheffield both to pursue a new job and to further my political activities.

I was working as a community development officer in some of the run-down housing estates in Sheffield, and was spreading the gospel among council tenants about how to organise and revolt against the local authority. I well remember that I made myself an early enemy there in the shape of Roy Hattersley's mother, who was a local councillor. She told me in no uncertain terms that people like me were not needed, nor were we helping the problems. Strange that her son should now share that opinion!

The job lasted six months and in 1975 I came home to take up a similar position with Knowsley Borough Council. It was at that time that I finally found the outlet for which unconsciously I had been searching: Militant.

The man who was to take me into Militant was Tony Mulhearn. It was a move which would change my whole political career and indeed my life. Looking back it was just as well that Tony and I met when we did. Had he not come along I might not even have stayed inside the Labour Party as I did. I was totally frustrated.

Tony Mulhearn and I had met before. As on many occasions since, the first time we met, a year earlier, while I was working at the Bronte, we had a fierce argument. I had gone to the council offices to lobby for a rent strike which I was organising against the council, and came face to face with Tony, who was even then on the District Labour Party executive committee. I had lashed out at him, demanding to know what kind of a Labour Party it was in which he was involved. Then I stormed off in a fearsome temper.

Tony Mulhearn well remembered that row the next time we met after a ward meeting in Wavertree and the two of us went off for a drink at a pub nearby.

In those days of course, in 1975, Militant did not have the numbers, or the influence, that it has now. I had come across the loony left – the shouters, the screamers, the agitators –

28

but as far as I was concerned they had nothing to say to the ordinary working man. It was nonsense.

Now Tony Mulhearn sat there in the pub and told me there was a group, centred around the *Militant* newspaper, which said and believed all the things I did. It spoke the language I understood. I think I could have jumped up and hugged him there and then. I had never read the paper, never read the books. I was an activist. I just wanted to get on with it, but here was was someone actually crystallising all the things I had been thinking, and telling me he agreed.

More than that, Liverpool was Militant's natural home. Like Tony Mulhearn, many of its leaders came from Liverpool – Labour Party supporters whose upbringing in many cases was in a city which even twenty years ago bore all the hallmarks of deprivation and urban neglect, symptoms which would get worse not better.

Once a great seaport, with its wealth based on the cotton, tobacco and slave trade, the Port of Liverpool had found itself stranded on the wrong side of the country. It sat facing the Atlantic and the Americas. By the time the sixties came round trade was switching to Europe, and the shipping lines which had once thronged the banks of the Mersey were moving their vessels to the likes of Felixstowe and Southampton. With them went industry. And with all of that went jobs.

The dole queues were growing. The Tories had no answers, and those on the Left of the Labour Party knew that until true Socialist policies were followed, that until the doctrines of Marx and Trotsky were implemented, there could be no solutions in a capitalist society where the catch-phrase "You've never had it so good" was already a byword. In that kind of climate, support for Militant could only thrive.

What they were saying to me then – and what Militant says today – is very little different from the things which Keir Hardie said when he founded the Labour Party. For example our philosophy of taking control of the means of production is essentially Clause Four of the Labour Party's constitution. Our aim is to keep as many supporters as

29

possible within the Labour Party to go down the road with us.

Marx said: "It is a Socialist's job to organise." Militant have proved that no one can organise as well as they can. Little wonder that having seen the efforts of those with whom I had worked in London to overthrow authority thwarted by a failure to organise, I found an immediate affinity with an organisation which was prepared to set out and carefully plan a political solution to the problems – no matter how long that plan might take in coming to fruition.

When I talk about Marxism, or Militant, I am talking about an exact political science, not what someone would, or would not, like to do. I am not talking of someone suddenly waking up to an idea and deciding to do it, but looking at the history of capitalist society as we know it, and the history of the Industrial Revolution.

We are talking about how to ensure that human beings are able to live in the future in peace, and with some sort of hope for a decent life. We are saying that if capitalism cannot provide that, and clearly it has failed to do so, then we have to offer the alternative.

That is not to say you want capitalism to succeed, or you want it to fail. That is not the issue. It is a question of what can, and cannot, exist. If you accept, as I do – and there are lots of facts and figures to support the argument – that capitalism is on the decline, then you have to decide what to put in its place. It is no good trying to reform a bankrupt system. That is the job of the Tories. I don't want to be a Socialist running a capitalist system. No one can run capitalism better than a capitalist. But even they are making a bad job of it because the system is crumbling.

You can make some reforms, but they can only be of benefit if behind them is a political philosophy. That is the important lesson to be learned from what we did in Liverpool. In some ways we were ahead of our time, but what we were doing was to build up ideas and individuals around the Labour and trade union movements. To organise for the

30

future. Those organisations will be there when the next stage comes.

It was once said by Marx that there were only two choices in his day – Socialism or Barbarism. Today the choice is Socialism or nuclear annihilation. Unless we can build up our organisation particularly in the western world there is nothing which will prevent this rotten system blowing itself apart.

Militant on Merseyside is unique. Elsewhere in the country Militant supporters may be accused of being Johnnie-come-latelies, but in Liverpool the Left has had Militant working from within as a component part for twenty-five to thirty years. Peter Taaffe, Pat Wall, Tony Mulhearn, Ted Mooney, Terry Harrison – Militant activists from the early days – all come from Liverpool backgrounds.

That is not to say that Militant cannot work elsewhere. We have proved it can, but it works in different ways, and with greater difficulties. In Liverpool, because of its history, it has been able to work behind a front of solidarity.

That's why I still laugh when I hear the nonsense talked about Militant's entryism into the Labour Party. No matter what you think of the politics of it, the fact is that the Derek Hattons, the Tony Mulhearns, were born and bred on Merseyside, and so was Militant. We've hardly tunnelled in or parachuted down.

Tony is a powerful man in every sense of the word. Some people feel intimidated by the stocky little figure who often gives the impression of being dour and humourless. Nothing could be further from the truth. Once you get to know him Tony is a very gentle and caring person but he doesn't suffer fools gladly – particularly political fools. All his working life he has been a staunch worker within the Labour Party, and through his job in the print industry a tireless campaigner for the trade unions, especially the National Graphical Association. It was no accident that on that evening in the pub he was able to talk with such authority about Militant and its aims and objectives. After all he was a founder member of the editorial board of the *Militant* newspaper.

He came from a traditional Liverpool Catholic family and went into the printing trade straight from school. Tony's concern for those out of work was probably rooted in the fact his own father spent years on the dole. He first joined the Labour Party in 1963. Two years later he was already serving on the District Labour Party and by 1973, at the age of thirty-four, was vice-president of the District Labour Party.

While Tony Mulhearn was the man who introduced me to Militant, the man who has had the greatest influence on my political thinking, and on the way in which we shaped our policy in Liverpool, was Peter Taaffe, one of the five members of the *Militant* editorial board expelled in the purge of February 1983. Soon after Tony and I discussed Militant, he took me to a contact meeting. These are gatherings to which dedicated Militants will invite anyone they believe supports their cause and is on the "good Left".

Peter Taaffe was there. His influence within Militant is legendary. He is the editor of *Militant* and like so many other Militants was born and bred on Merseyside. Peter came from Birkenhead, and worked for a time in the treasurer's department of Liverpool City Council. To this day there is no other single individual whose political brain has so impressed me. I am convinced that he is the greatest political thinker I have ever met, and has no equal where political strategies and tactics are concerned.

We first met in Stanley House, which was then one of Militant's meeting places in Liverpool. Bear in mind that the numbers in Militant across the country at that time were small, yet even then the meeting attracted fifty or sixty people. Taaffe was the principal speaker. I remember hanging on his every word. He told us that even though we had a Labour Government, it was our job to stay inside the Party, and change it from within. We had to make the Labour Party the party we wanted it to be. Peter Taaffe made me realise that I could become part of the mainstream of politics, but at the same time be part of a revolutionary change. It was all the things I had been trying to say for years, from the very first time I started

32

getting involved with Christianity and trying to find answers there.

From that point in 1975 I became more and more involved. I sold papers on the streets, spoke on platforms at meetings, and tried to influence and convince other people of the merits of Militant. From that time on we began to have a greater and greater influence on politics in Merseyside. I met more and more people who embraced the idea, and who found the same answers for which I had been looking.

From the moment I joined in, it was a total commitment, because that's the way I am. Unless I am totally involved in something, then I don't want to be a part of it – especially where something which is so important and so fundamental to me is concerned. So from then on I lived and breathed Militant. There has been nothing else in my life. I have involved my family in that commitment, and Militant has influenced and guided everything I have done politically.

One of the most popular political games in Britain at the present is Militant-bashing. We have been used as a stick with which to beat the Labour Party, and, particularly in Liverpool, as an excuse for the worst excesses of the Tories in their attempts to emasculate local government.

It's perhaps not surprising then, in a climate where any discussions about Militant start from the standpoint of doing a hatchet job, that we have been portrayed as dangerous subversives whose very existence threatens the nation. Be it the press, or the likes of Michael Crick, in his book *Militant*, we have been the subject of so-called "exposés" designed, it seems, to prove that we are a sinister secret party.

So what is this evidence? That we are a potent political force in Britain today? That, as Crick himself acknowledges, we became the fifth strongest political group in the country? That we are capable of organising and orchestrating our plans in a number of ways which are the envy of the Labour Party as a whole?

All of these things are true. As for being a secret society operating within the Labour Party, I can only say that it is the media themselves who have created this myth, when faced with a group of people who don't spend their time blabbing about their activities, but get on with the job. The press have been willing collaborators in the campaign against us, and few journalists have bothered to ask what the real truth is.

The truth about Militant is, ironically, best summarised in a passage by journalist Julie Burchill, writing in the *Mail on Sunday*. "Militant cannot be stopped by a few expulsions, because it is a religion the way Labour used to be, and the way Thatcherism is," she wrote. "These Marxist fundamentalists have all the anger, hatred, pride and passion that Labour threw out with Michael Foot's bathwater. If Mrs Thatcher is the only man in the Cabinet, they are the only men in the Labour Party. Only if the march of Militant continues will Mrs Thatcher find opponents worthy of her."

So what is the truth about the battle for Liverpool Town Hall, the role of Militant, and my involvement with Militant? Until now there had been no opportunity for a leading Militant voice to speak up, without his or her words and views being distorted by a hostile press. My own account should help put that record straight.

I was not cast in the Militant mould the media wanted. My lifestyle didn't fit their blinkered view. I have a pleasant home, an attractive wife and four bright kids, two of whom enjoy riding horses. I have a nice car, take holidays abroad, and enjoy a busy social life – be it night-clubbing with friends, or going to a football match. I wear good clothes, enjoy good food and the occasional drink. In short, my politics apart, I am far too close for comfort to my critics.

I was an ordinary Liverpudlian, with a perhaps more than generous helping of the wit and arrogance with which most Scousers are blessed, but all of those things were my strengths, not my weaknesses. They helped me achieve what I did, and that was where the resentment set in. I was an ordinary man catapulted into the limelight, and not the unimaginative, sackcloth-and-ashes Socialist they would have preferred.

The press went to town on me, and you could almost hear people saying: "That's not the way we expect Militants to behave." Never, locally, or nationally, has Militant ever said that.

The only thing that is expected of us, no matter what the lifestyle we lead, is that we make regular contributions to the cause. I have given money to Militant, and make no apologies for it. Never a week has gone by in the last fifteen years in which I have not given money, and I shall go on doing so.

There is no standard amount, no set subscription. Some people have talked of a "levy" of ten per cent of income. That is simply not true. Certainly I have not given that much, but you are expected to make a financial sacrifice. Contrary to the media myths and legends Militant doesn't get money from Russian gold, and it certainly doesn't get it from big business, for obvious reasons.

Its income comes from the sales of its books and papers, and from those, like me, who support it. There are some individuals in Militant, for whom I have nothing but respect and admiration, who give far more than I ever have. Some who give less can less afford it.

Some people actually reach the position where they live on the breadline because of their commitment to the ideas of Militant. That is certainly true of some of those who work full time for Militant. I respect that too, though it is something I could never do myself, but I would be very critical of someone who got involved with Militant, yet was not prepared to make the sacrifice of money as well as the sacrifice of time and effort.

But my first real success as a Militant activist was in Knowsley, a town of 194,000 people on the outskirts of Liverpool. Having returned from Sheffield I was now doing a very similar job back on my own doorstep as community development officer with Knowsley Borough Council.

My job was to liaise with local community associations and groups of tenants in Kirkby, a huge overspill area, where in the 1960s, as old houses in Liverpool came down, people had moved out from the city on the promise and expectation of a better lifestyle in new homes. The reality was very different. The tower blocks and high-rise homes brought their own problems, and the houses which were supposed to have been the Promised Land became, in many cases, modern slums. The town planners had worked on facts and figures, and the problems that people would face in their new environment had taken second place. New building systems spawned the problems of damp and condensation, old people found themselves living in tower blocks where the lifts frequently broke down, and heating bills were a constant nightmare.

Not only that, but while new homes had been built little thought had been given to providing the community with places where people could get together socially, and there was very little in the way of recreation areas for children in a town which was ultimately to have more youngsters of school age than any other new town in Western Europe.

Against this background the borough council saw my role as one in which I would involve the local authority at grass-roots level with the tenants. I saw things very differently and decided that what I should really be doing as a community development officer was to help the campaign for more resources.

Once again I was in conflict with the very people who employed me. Those arguments went on from the very start. The council said I was working against them and not for them, but after a couple of years we settled our differences and they tacitly accepted my redefinition of my job.

While all this was going on in 1975 I had joined the local government officers' union, NALGO. My early experiences with Militant had taught me even then that the trade unions were a vital part of the machinery to change society and could be a very important power base.

It became clear to me that the Knowsley branch of NALGO was ripe for change. I found myself an ally in the shape of a lad called Roger Bannister, who was involved with the Young Socialists at that time and who was also in NALGO. Then there was Irene Buxton who in later years regrettably was to become a Militant turncoat – denouncing me and Militant in a Granada TV *World In Action* programme and giving evidence at the Labour party inquiry into Militant.

We often met in a local pub in Knowsley, and spent hour after hour talking about NALGO, and how we could drag the local branch away from the right-wing professionals who ran it, into its real role – as a hard-Left active trade union. So every time an issue came up, no matter whether it was regrading, or simply plans to take on outside consultants, the three of us became closely involved in leading the fight. People soon came to recognise us for what we were, and more and more of them wanted to join. Roger and Irene had not started out as Militant supporters, but they were soon fully committed, and ultimately Roger was one of those who was expelled.

As result of continuous effort we worked our way into the union. I became chairman, Roger the deputy chairman and Irene the branch secretary. There was also Ray Andrews, a Cockney who had not been in Knowsley very long, but who was very much a part of the discussions. It was a textbook operation. The branch consisted of professional right-wing white-collar workers who were only interested in the union to safeguard their jobs, and for the sports and leisure activities it offered.

Then there was a whole network of lowly paid NALGO workers who had never been organised, and who were simply waiting for someone to come along and lead them in the battle against the borough council for better pay and conditions. Before too long more and more of them became Militant supporters. It was the classic case of Militant working from within. From there our influence spread out to the rest of the trade union movement, selling papers, attracting more and more converts. It became an important training ground for Militant on Merseyside.

It was an especially important area for involving young people, who had never been able to articulate their ideas before, and who, once introduced to Militant, saw what they really wanted politically.

Knowsley NALGO never looked back, and became an example to the rest of the trade union movement. We proved that it was possible to take on local authority employers and win better conditions. We fought against departmental cuts in staffing and won. We also forged links with the community associations and the tenants' groups in the town and with other local authority trade unions in the borough. We worked together and campaigned together. They were the kind of lessons which I would later take with me into Liverpool City Council. And from a personal point of view I had built up a position of power which Knowsley Borough Council would have found very difficult to challenge even had they tried.

So now, by 1975, I was part of Militant and part of the Labour Party. Whatever the constitution, the truth is that Militant's ideas are rooted within the Labour Party, not just in Liverpool, but elsewhere. The role of a Militant is to work within the Labour Party. It doesn't matter whether it's Knowsley North, or Bradford. It doesn't matter how bad the constituency party may be. The job is to stay in there, and influence events. It is a case of ensuring that you change the organisation from within. There are all too many stupid revolutionary groups on the fringes of the party who have never done a thing, never can do anything and never will do anything.

It seemed during all that time that I was never at home. There were meetings most nights, whether it happened to be a trade union meeting or a gathering of local tenants to campaign for better housing conditions, and of course there were Militant meetings. The weekends would see me out on the streets selling the *Militant* newspaper.

But nothing could take away the sheer personal joy I felt when our son Ben was born on November 16th, 1975. Like every father I desperately wanted a son – and Shirley had her work cut out to stop me going out and buying his first pair of football boots there and then!

With Becky still only less than two years old, and now Ben on the scene, life at home seemed like a constant round of changing nappies. I always did my bit – Shirley always says that bottoms were my speciality! But she was behind me all the way in my political ambitions and never begrudged the time that it took out of our social life.

Those ambitions gave me a real chance to show what Militant could do when in 1978 I was asked to stand for the council. Liverpool had a strange political pedigree. Back in the 1950s it had been controlled by the Tories. Then in the great days of old-fashioned Labour politicians like Bessie Braddock it was a Labour stronghold. There was a strong Liberal influence too, which, as the local Labour Party declined, became more important. By 1974 at the time of local government reorganisation the Liberals had taken control of the city council and held it in a stranglehold.

So by 1978 when my chance to run for office came along the opposition Labour group were weak, right wing, and completely demoralised. It was the perfect chance for Militant. Activists like myself and Tony Mulhearn – who for four years by that time had been vice-president – had built up a powerful position of influence within the District Labour Party.

At national level there is the Labour Party and its policy-forming body the National Executive Committee. At local level there are the constituency Labour parties, made up of local ward parties. Within local councils are the Labour groups – the elected Labour councillors, be they in control of the local authority or in opposition.

The District Labour Party in each town is the forum in which every Labour Party member can exchange views and push forward policies which they believe their elected representatives on the council should be following.

But we intended that the DLP should be more than a paper tiger. It was our intention to make it the body which formulated policy for Liverpool's Labour councillors. We would build up a power base which would finally be so important that we controlled the Labour group. They would not be able to make a move without us.

My chance came in Tuebrook ward, where I had been working for years on the ground for Militant. It had always been a solid Liberal seat, but they decided to ditch the then Labour candidate, Dave Mitchell, who was very much a right-winger, and selected me in his place. Every left-winger who cared threw in their lot with us, to prove to the old right-wing that the seat was winnable.

The buzz I got from it was *The Merchant of Venice* all over again. I loved knocking on doors, and arguing the toss with the voters. The excitement was incredible. I had the opportunity to put into action all the things I had been saying. Tuebrook was certainly my political launching pad.

Shirley was very much a part of it. She went round on the doorsteps with me, and to this day one of the funny little moments which sticks in my mind is the row we had with our daughter Becky over the red rosette we wanted to pin on her. She was only four, but even then she had decided that she was an Everton "Blues" supporter. So there was no way she would allow Shirley to pin a red rosette on her, and rode round in her buggy all day without one!

It was true that the people I met didn't know what Militant was then. What swung it was the fact they had not seen a Labour candidate knocking on their door and staging street-corner meetings for years. They loved it.

It was a three-cornered fight and when the votes were counted, the Liberals who held the seat were wiped out. The Tory candidate, John Irving, won – but only by a tiny majority of ninety-one. You would have thought from the celebrations afterwards that we had won!

The following year, 1979, I indicated that I was quite prepared to stand in Tuebrook again, but in Netherley, not far from my home, a councillor was standing down in the Woolton East ward and they asked me to stand in his place. It meant so much to be canvassing in an area where I had grown up and where the friends I had mixed with over the years still lived.

My job in Netherley wasn't to persuade people to join us, but to grab those who were already there. So I became heavily

40

involved in the campaign by the flat-dwellers, families whose homes were three- and four-storey walk-up blocks which were a disgrace. The conditions they had to live in were appalling. (Mind you, to this day no one realises that during a six-month spell in 1970, after leaving the fire service and waiting to take up my place on the college course in London, I worked as a builder's labourer – and one of the jobs I worked on was the building of those flats in Netherley!) Once again I put my Militant background to work, and began to get more and more of the flat-dwellers involved with the ideas of the organisation. There were a few other Militants in the ward already, and between us we began to build up the support.

When it came to polling day the result was never in doubt. In a four-cornered fight against the Liberals, the Tories and a Communist candidate I topped the poll with a majority of 3,614. What was more important was that on that day I became one of four Militants elected to the city council. The others were Pauline Dunlop, Julie Taylor and Peter Lloyd.

That was the day we began to translate Socialist theory into practice. Until then the right wing had controlled the Labour group, but the votes of the four of us made all the difference, and the Left were able to take over.

I started out as a backbencher, but within six months we had begun to establish ourselves, and caused uproar by opposing our own group. It was, ironically, a budget debate in which Labour were recommending a fifty per cent increase in rates in order to balance the council budget. Nine of us got together, ignored the Whip, and proposed only thirteen per cent. John Hamilton, the leader, was furious when he heard what we were plotting. Another right-winger threatened to have us disciplined.

I laughed in his face and suggested that in that case he might like to take us in front of the District Labour Party. That was an end of it, because he knew, as did everyone else inside the Labour group, that it was now the DLP which made policy and controlled the machine.

The Labour group was being forced to change under the influence and power of the District Party. Within the Labour and trade union movements Tony Mulhearn and the other Militant leading figures had been building the base. Now it was ours. What the Labour group said didn't make a blind bit of difference.

Our hand was strengthened by the election of 1979. It was the start of the Thatcher years and no city the length and breadth of Britain was to feel the impact of her policies more keenly than Liverpool. A once great city was already in decline and had been neglected even by Labour. Miles and miles of docks which had once bustled with life stood idle as a testament to the shift in world trade. Industry was moving away and the dole queues were growing. There was to be no help from Thatcher for inner-city Liverpool. Under Margaret Thatcher's policy of "free market forces" there was to be no pump priming. The new sunrise industries from the world of high technology would not be directed to areas like Liverpool to solve its problems. Instead they were to be allowed to go where they would, grabbing the best grants and cash handouts.

There had always been a North–South divide. Now the rift was widening. The fat cats of the Conservative Party didn't give a damn about Liverpool, and the Tory press painted a picture of a militant work force whose strike record was really at the root of the trouble. They never stopped to say that Liverpool's problems were the same problems being felt in the North-East or in South Wales. The difference was that Liverpudlians in their own bitter, articulate way could hit out at injustice and inequality in a manner which has always grabbed the headlines.

The tension and resentment, which was to explode in the face of the government with the first Toxteth riots, mounted. When the lid blew off Toxteth in 1981 no one could believe it – not even those of us so close to Liverpool and its many problems that we knew the bitterness simmering beneath the surface. Toxteth was not about blacks versus whites. After all, the majority of the blacks who live in that area are third-generation Liverpudlians who have more right to their place in our city than many of the white families who have moved in from other parts of the country. They live, by one of the ironies of fate, in streets which once housed the captains of industry and the sea-faring men who grew wealthy on the slave trade which brought many West Indians to Liverpool. But throughout the centuries those elegant houses at the top of the hill above the Mersey have been allowed to fall into squalor and decay. They became bedsitters and flats where, in many cases, the unscrupulous landlords of the Rachman era, grew fat on the backs of the desperate and the poor.

Toxteth by 1981 was a ghetto – for the poor, and the deprived, black and white alike. It inevitably attracted criminal elements and to survive in the streets of Toxteth you had at very least to live on your wits.

The police did not help. Their policies at that time in Toxteth were heavy-handed and aggressive. Their response to outbreaks of trouble in the area was to swamp the district with snatch squads whose style was to arrest first and ask questions afterwards.

Politically we in the Labour Party won many converts in the area but all their cries for help fell on deaf ears at the Town Hall where the Liberal administration had not even begun to recognise the size of the problem.

The riots themselves, when they came, were horrific. No one who was there can seek to justify them. There was violence on an unprecedented scale. And once it began it was self-perpetuating. It was almost as though no single individual felt held accountable and that there was a collective responsibility for the looting, burning and torching which set the area ablaze night after night.

I know those streets well – places like Upper Parliament Street and Granby Street where I stood watching buildings which were Liverpool landmarks razed to the ground. The Racquets Club in Upper Parliament Street – the preserve of elitist generations of Liverpool businessmen – was reduced to ashes in a night. The old Rialto cinema building on the corner of Princes Road, with its distinctive domes, was burned to the ground in hours. Cars overturned and blazing, hostile crowds hurling bricks and petrol bombs and lines of grim-faced police-men beating out Zulu-like battle rhythms on their riot shields became the daily sights and sounds in Toxteth.

The riots had begun on July 3rd, 1981. Three days later, on July 6th, for the first time on the mainland in Britain, the police used gas canisters to dispel the mobs. The rioting spread through Lodge Lane and Park Road and rate-payers were lat-er to be told that the bill for damage could reach £10 million. Hundreds of police officers were called in from all over the North when the riots flared again at the end of that month. This time the troubles claimed their first victim, a twenty-two year old cripple who was knocked down by a police van and died, as hostile crowds and the police fought each other in the area.

By the beginning of August the smoke had cleared, and the city and the Government began to count the cost.

The man ultimately appointed to try and come to terms with Liverpool and its problems was Michael Heseltine, who in the wake of the riots was given his role as Minister for Merseyside.

Meantime we in the Labour Party and in Militant had other battles to fight as Liverpool tried to settle back into something like normality. That autumn in 1981 the rows over the reorganisation of secondary education were reaching their climax.

Ten years of working amongst the rank and file of the Labour movement were complete for Militant on Merseyside. The battle over education gave us the perfect opportunity to demonstrate our power in practical terms. Year by year we had pushed the District Labour Party to the Left. Now in November 1981 a school called Croxteth would give us the perfect springboard for victory.

F O U R

THE BATTLE FOR CROXTETH

Of all the battles which Militant fought in Liverpool, one stands as the watershed. It began before we ever came to power, but without it we might never have taken control when we did. It was the battle for Croxteth Community School. Its importance in the history of Militant in Liverpool, and in the history of the District Labour Party, must never be underestimated or forgotten.

It was an object lesson in how to organise and politicise a whole community through a local campaign. It won us more supporters than any other single fight we took on, and swelled the ranks of Militant.

My concern about education was not just based on my own experiences at the Liverpool Institute and the shortcomings I had personally experienced in the grammar school system. By now in November 1981 I had children of my own of school age. Becky was seven, and going to Mosspits Lane Primary School down the road from our home in Thingwall Road, Wavertree, the house to which we had moved some years before and where we live to this day. Ben was five and attending the same school. Our second daughter, Sarah, born on January 10th, 1978, was three, and I had just become a proud Dad for the fourth time with the birth of Laura on April 25th, 1981. So Derek Hatton in his role as family man had a vested interest in the kind of education that Liverpool offered to its youngsters.

The Liberals controlled the city council, but plans for reorganising secondary education, as the Secretary of State had demanded, were a shambles. For two years they had been floating plans to close down four secondary schools, to deal with the problem of the falling number of pupils, and they had identified some of the schools by name.

On Tuesday afternoon, November 10th, 1981, the plan was due to go before the Education Sub-Committee, but before they ever met the news leaked. Croxteth Community School was on the list. The school had first opened in September 1956 as Croxteth Secondary Modern for Girls. Just over ten years later it merged with Croxteth Boys' Secondary Modern to become Croxteth Comprehensive.

The idea that it should be closed was a bolt from the blue. There had never been a suggestion that the school might shut. Now it was scheduled to be closed down by July 1982. The reaction was instantaneous. Parents flooded into the school demanding to know if the news was true.

It took them about a week to organise a public meeting, and initially it was the headmaster and the teachers who were behind it. As the protests grew, roles changed, and soon it was the parents as a body who were calling the tune.

They organised themselves into a Parents' Action Committee, though some of the leading campaigners were the pupils themselves. Among them was a sixth-former called Collette D'Arcy, who became, in the years that followed, a convert to the Militant cause, and a tireless worker inside the Town Hall for the Labour council when we came to power.

At the very outset she set about organising the campaign among the sixth-formers, and soon she was acting as a go-between for the teachers and the parents. Her father, as secretary of the action committee, was involved in the campaign of civil disobedience, as the parents blocked off streets, stopped the traffic and staged demonstrations.

The teachers could not be seen to be willing parties to that aspect of the fight, so Collette became the link between the two sides, so that they could co-ordinate their action.

The energy and effort which went into the early months of the campaign were an inspiration. The Croxteth community was determined to keep its school, and there were no lengths to which they would not go to make their point. Meantime the council machinery was grinding on. The proposal to shut down the school went to the full Education Committee to be ratified, and finally was steam-rollered through with little or no discussion.

Still the community refused to accept what was happening. They lobbied the Department of Education, wrote letters and held public meetings. But there was to be no reprieve. The school was to close on July 16th, 1982. The Liberals were determined, and so was the Education Minister, Sir Keith Joseph, who three days before the school was to be shut arrived in the city to talk with the local council about their much-delayed reorganisation plans.

Parents from the school lobbied his visit, and pleaded with him to change his mind. Outside the Liverpool Polytechnic the "Save Croxteth Comprehensive" demonstrators gathered, with banners which read "Sir Thief Joseph". Two eggs were thrown and narrowly missed him. Sir Keith, while he said he would look again at the parents' case, said he could make no promises. It was the last straw.

That afternoon, at four o'clock, as the 400 pupils filed out of classes, a group of carefully organised parents, about forty of whom had been picketing the school, walked into the school buildings in Stonebridge Lane and Parkstile Lane and occupied them. Schools throughout the city were due to close

47

for the summer, and there were clearly those who believed this would only be a token occupation, and that the battle for Croxteth would come to a natural close.

Anyone who thought that, had underestimated the strength of feeling in the community, and the political forces gathering. Collette D'Arcy's father, Cyril, who had been elected secretary of the action group, had laid his plans carefully, helped by his daughter. Another leading light was Phil Knibb, later to play a key role in the campaign. This was to be no seven-day wonder, but a strategically planned take-over. Sleeping bags, blankets and supplies of hot drinks were taken into the school. Cyril, who also had two other children on the register at Croxteth, worked out "occupation rotas", right down to night watchmen, to prevent council officials moving in and reclaiming the premises.

The Liberal spokesman for education on the city council, Richard Kemp, was quoted in the media locally as saying: "There is no possibility of the school being there as a school in September. We have plans for the youth wing to be used by the Manpower Services Commission to try to alleviate the chronic youth unemployment in the area. But as a school the building must close. I believe the vast majority of parents have accepted our decision."

Never has anything been further from the truth.

The campaign of civil disobedience continued. At one stage the parents marched into the studios of Liverpool's independent radio station, Radio City, threatening to occupy the building unless they were given time to air their grievances. They won their platform. On August 2nd, 1982 Michael Heseltine, then the Minister for Merseyside, visited the city, and was pelted with eggs and tomatoes by Croxteth protestors.

But the campaign badly needed political muscle, and it was about to get it, from Militant, the Labour Party and the trade unions. All kind of fringe elements tried to get in on the act, the Communist Party, the Workers' Revolutionary Party, the Socialist Workers' Party all turned out: the trendies who try to get on the bandwagon of every campaign. They, however, do

48

not know how to organise, while Militant on Merseyside knew even then what was needed. Local ward activists involved themselves in the campaign.

We pressed at constituency party level for more positive backing. The local Labour Party Young Socialists – the young Militants – went onto the streets, and onto the doorsteps. Letters were sent to the Labour Party locally and nationally. Meetings were lobbied. The campaign was given a transfusion of new blood. The community was politicised, and the resolve was born that Croxteth School would not die. It would reopen at the start of the new term: the community had taken over the school. Now they would run it.

Looking back it seems like an impossible goal. Where would they get the money? Where would they get the materials, where would they find the teachers? It didn't matter, because the will was there, and that kind of political will can achieve almost anything. The people of Croxteth had some of the worst housing conditions in the country at that time. They had forty per cent unemployment. They had no sports centre, no leisure facilities. What they did have was a school which was the heart of their community, and they were not about to give it up without a fight. More than that, they planned to use it for the benefit of the community. It would become not just a place of learning which opened at 9 in the morning and closed at 3:30 in the afternoon, standing empty and unused for the rest of the time. It would become a centre not just for schooling, but for all the recreational, social and adult educational facilities which they had been denied.

What's more, helped by the support now being shown them by Militant and the trade unions, they were returning to the Labour Party as active workers, and woe betide any local councillors who didn't fall in line and positively back them.

It was decided that Croxteth Free Community School would open its doors on September 20th, 1982 and, when it did, more than 350 pupils, twice the number expected, reported for lessons. It was an astonishing sight. Children who had never worn school uniforms in their lives turned up kitted out in regulation school blazers, trousers or skirts and ties. Such was the pride of the parents.

The staff of nine teachers were all volunteers, some of them unemployed teachers from as far afield as London and Scotland, who had read of the campaign and asked if they could join in. Ironically many of them had better qualifications than their predecessors. The parents' selection committee saw to that. They also ensured that the teachers who were selected were politically acceptable. A governing body had been elected and teachers who wanted to join them – even though it was on an unpaid basis – faced a very critical selection procedure.

It mattered not a jot to the parents that the people they were interviewing outranked them academically. They wanted commitment, and they were conscious of the fact that while the teachers were only being appointed on a voluntary basis, they wanted to select people who would stay on when the school was taken back into the public sector. What's more they didn't want Liberal and Tory trendies, who could not accept the political implications of the fight.

The problems the school faced were monumental: electricity supplies would be cut, oil for heating the buildings was limited, and winter was setting in. The Liberal administration looked on, and took a decision that conditions would eventually "starve" the parents out. They reinforced their siege mentality by threatening to send in the bailiffs and the electricity board even tried to cut off supplies.

Nothing they did could break the resolve of the Croxteth community, and, to the embarrassment of the authorities, the school not only stayed open, but thrived. The school roll had settled down to between 150 and 200 pupils, and even though official supplies were stopped, school meals went on, cooked and served by local women and provided free.

Phil Knibb was appointed as the co-ordinating headmaster. He had no teaching qualifications, but that was never the intention. His job was to manage the whole operation, and before long he was joined by another man who was to help bolster Militant philosophy in the area, his brother, George

Knibb. His role was typical of that of many of the parents, who sat in alongside teachers during classes to maintain discipline, and continuity; involvement was important in a situation where teachers changed from week to week, sometimes even from day to day.

Discipline was George's speciality. There was no question of corporal punishment in the formal sense of the word, but in many cases in the senior classes you were dealing with teenagers who could give as good as they got, and who had been brought up in the school of hard knocks. Sometimes the only thing they understood was a clip round the ear, to remind them who was in charge. With youngsters like that, most of them facing life on the dole, it was important too that they understood the real world and how it worked. So lessons in maths and social studies took on a whole new perspective.

I well remember George telling me how one afternoon, with a shortage of teachers, he himself went in to teach maths to the fifth form. He was met with a barrage of abuse from kids who claimed they had no books or paper, and could not go on with their lessons. As ever there was one ringleader, who gave George a particularly difficult time. George simply went over, clipped him round the ear, and told him in no uncertain terms, that if he didn't like the way things were being run, then he could leave. The boy left and brought his father back to school, but it was typical that when his father heard what had happened he too clipped the lad round the ear and went home.

Maths lessons were, though, a problem for George, who had no academic qualifications whatever. Then he hit on the solution. Instead of discussing abstract mathematical equations he began to relate the subject to the kind of world in which the senior pupils would shortly find themselves, either at work, or on the dole. Those kinds of discussions soon, of course, became political debates in which the ideology of the Labour Party, the Tories, the Liberals – and by contrast that of Militant – were questioned. Many of the youngsters could not accept that George and others were giving their time for nothing. It was outside their understanding. They believed that he must

51

be earning at least £100 a week. To convince them required a political explanation, and it was not long before many of them began to understand and support the ideals of Militant, towards which George himself was already moving.

I suppose the classic example of the way in which those teen-agers became politicised was the project they set up themselves to help swell the school funds. They raised the cash to buy a badge machine, and started producing and selling badges for rallies and demonstrations. No wonder the Liberals and the Tory education ministers started getting twitchy. The badges, produced by a so-called non-political school, carried slogans like: "Thatcher Out" and "Ditch the Bitch!"

On another occasion they had became so involved in the fund-raising that kids who were taking their CSE in cookery decided to use their parents as guinea pigs, and organised a dinner at the school one evening at £2.50 a head. They invited the entire action committee, and laid on wine as well.

After dinner the committee had gone across the road to their local pub, the Lobster, to enjoy a few drinks. Normally at least two pickets would have been left on duty, but as it was almost Christmas, and everyone was in the mood to celebrate, they left the place unmanned for a couple of hours.

In that time someone broke in and stole the television and video, which were particularly important as teaching aids: in the absence of teachers even an unqualified parent could go into a class and use them. The teaching tapes, which were also stolen, were the parents' lifeline on the days when teachers, who were either unemployed or in part-time work, were not able to turn up for lessons.

This was one of the moments when the pressures became so great that the parents almost threw their hand in. Over that Christmas and into 1983 their backs were to the wall. The weather was a major factor. It was cold, and there were heavy rains, and it had reached the stage where children would arrive from home, soaking wet, and then spend the day sitting in their wet clothes in cold unheated classrooms. Before long absenteeism began to take its toll.

Support from the parents began to dwindle. They would hand over donations, but told the committee that with conditions as they were they could not continue to send their children into school. The crisis worsened and by January 1983 things had reached rock bottom. The parents held an emergency meeting and it was decided that they could only last out for another week. It had reached the stage where the same people who were teaching and helping at the school during the day were then spending the nights sleeping on the floor to maintain the occupation. The decision to give in reduced many of them to tears.

It was at this stage that Militant came into its own. What was needed more than anything was practical help and political backing. The Labour Party Young Socialists – the young wing of Militant – moved in and provided just that. They addressed the emergency meeting, and paved the way for a whole new initiative. They went out on the streets with buckets collecting money, and began the whole process of lobbying every possible political group on the Left through letters and meetings. They even approached local MPs for donations.

One of their first successes was to persuade the men at the Ford plant at Halewood to support the Croxteth parents, and a cheque came in for £500 to help buy oil for the heating, and food. Until then some members of the action committee had been sceptical. They had seen the activities of the Communists and the SWP as seven-day wonders. Why should Militant be any different? Once they saw the money rolling in, once they knew there was enough to buy food for school meals and warm classrooms, they went back into the campaign with renewed vigour and conviction.

Militant, from its London headquarters, sent people to help, and locally fellow councillor Felicity Dowling, Tony Mulhearn and I organised all the backing we could muster, culminating in a demonstration, march and rally.

In many ways the direct action of the take-over became secondary to the political action which was then taking place. The Parents' Action Committee had recognised that in the long term there would be no commitment to their ideas of education for the area unless a Labour council was to be elected. Tony Mulhearn and I had given assurances that if we were returned to power then the future of the school within whatever system we introduced would be guaranteed. So from the summer of 1982 the parents and the community were not only working to keep their school open, but were campaigning for a return to Labour rule which would guarantee its future.

In February 1983 the Liberals sent out a £27,000 bill for rates to the parents. Then they threatened to send in the bailiffs. But now the local elections were only months away, and Croxteth was part of the political battle.

Liverpool, under the Liberals, and on occasions when we in the Labour Party had held the balance of power, had for ten years been a Toytown of politics. Sometimes we refused to rule because they could block our decisions. Sometimes the Liberals tried to rule and we blocked their decisions. The see-saw politics at Liverpool Town Hall became a laughing stock. Only with a clear Labour majority to run the city could Militant, and the District Labour Party, be certain of gaining its objectives. We knew, if we were honest, that the chances of our taking total power in 1983 were slim. But with the backing of a lobby as vocal as the Croxteth community, and by using their experiences and their enthusiasm in the marginal seats, there was the chance that we might just win the day.

It was a brilliant tactic, and one which was to pay off. People would knock on doors and say: "We're from Croxteth Comprehensive – if you don't vote Labour we will be closed down." It had become such a live issue that it was a real vote-winner. Now people were aware that their fight was not just about the school, which we as a Labour group had promised to keep open as part of our own plans for the reorganisation of secondary education. It was about the broken promises for housing, libraries, sporting facilities, and the way in which deprived areas like Croxteth had been neglected.

So, come the election campaign the Croxteth community became a cavalcade on the road for Labour. They joined forces with the Militants, and the trade unionists who had backed them, and went out in massive numbers to win votes. Win votes they did – in the marginal seats we needed to take power.

Our victory at the polls was to be Croxteth's victory too – and the support the community gave us would not be forgotten. The school stayed open, and has to this day.

F I V E

DAYS OF REVOLUTION

It was Thursday night, May 5th, 1983. All day Shirley and I had been on the doorstep, drumming up support from Labour voters. Now the count was on, and the real battle for the future of Liverpool, and Militant, was about to begin. Not that we could have anticipated what was about to happen. We had boasted that we could take ten seats and decimate the Liberals. Privately we conceded that we could end up short of our target, and none of us really expected to take control that time around.

I had spent the whole evening in my own ward in Netherley, which, in local elections in Liverpool, is always one of the first results out of the bag. You don't count the votes there, you weigh them. Then I set out to drive into the city, to appear on Granada Television's local election programme. I shall always remember it, because it was the moment I knew we had finally succeeded. I was driving across the Churchill Way flyover, not a stone's throw from the council offices, listening to the results coming in on local radio, when I heard the news that we had taken Warbreck ward, the seat held by the Tory leader Reg Flude, and one we had never expected to win. Warbreck had always been either Tory or Liberal. It was years since Labour had won it. Our candidate there was Jimmy Hackett, but we all knew, or thought we knew, that his nomination was just a case of going through the motions. In theory, he should not have been in the running. But the Tory vote was beginning to crumble that year, as voters began to swing towards the Liberals. The split vote worked in our favour. Now they announced that Jimmy Hackett had taken the seat.

If anyone had seen me at that moment they would have been convinced I was mad. I let out a huge whoop, waved a clenched fist in the air and nearly lost control of the car. I knew then that there was nothing to stop us.

Now Militant could show what it was made of, and Liverpool, where the movement was born, could become a "show-piece" city, a platform on which to demonstrate what could be achieved.

When I arrived at the television studios, in the shadow of the Town Hall itself, there was no holding me. Sir Trevor Jones, leader of the Liberals, was there, and the defeated Tory leader, Reg Flude, who had agreed to appear never dreaming he would lose his seat. I could not contain myself. The results, as they came in, looked better and better, and the opposition looked grimmer and grimmer.

Hours later fellow Labour councillor Tony Byrne and I stood together, celebrating over a pint. What a night it had been! A whole carload of us had toured local Labour clubs on the way back to Netherley and we got there about two in the morning. For hours the two of us had stood side by side telling reporters and interviewers that we had always known we would win. Now the man, who over the next three years, as finance chairman, was to help shape the political future of Liverpool, turned to me and said, "What the hell are we going to do?"

We had taken fifty-one seats: nine from the Liberals, one from the SDP, and the Tory seat in Warbreck. But no one was more surprised than we were. We had planned the 1983 campaign as the final push. Now we were in power a full year earlier than any of us had anticipated.

I told him: "We're going to show the bastards what we're made of. We're going to do all the things we said we would. You are going to build houses. I am going to create jobs. It's going to be bloody marvellous."

Tony Byrne cuts an unlikely figure as a politician. While I am renowned for my snappy suits and smart appearance, Tony is just as well known for his sweat shirts, bomber jackets and trainers. He's a quietly spoken, lean, bustling man and with his bristly beard and balding head looks more like an ageing student than a successful politician. But his casual, almost scruffy appearance belies his astute political nature. Tony and I had first met in 1973 when I was at the Bronte Neighbourhood Centre and he a worker with a housing association. He joined the council at the age of forty-one in 1980, a year after I had first been elected. A former draughtsman with English Electric, he had been an active member of TASS, the Association of Technical and Supervisory Staff – though who would have guessed that a man who started life as a trainee Jesuit priest would go on to become a trade unionist and then a politician.

That night I knew that Tony shared with me the same ambitions to change life in Liverpool, but he did not share the Militant camp with me, and never has. But I thought to myself, "Not only are we going to change Liverpool, we are also going to prove what Militant is all about. The revolution starts here."

It must have been the only time a revolution began with a hangover. It was the celebration to end them all. We drank through until six in the morning, then I went home, had a shower, and turned up for breakfast television. Even then the celebrations continued. Everywhere I went people hoisted me onto their shoulders and chaired me around. The mood was incredible. How many people really believed we were going to fulfil our promises I don't know. But they did believe that a decade of Liberal and Tory neglect was gone and at last there was a chance. If they didn't know what was going to happen, at least they knew it was going to be different.

It was that same Friday morning that we walked into the municipal offices to take over. I had been the Labour spokesman on personnel for years, so I knew the Town Hall officials, and they knew me.

First I went to see Arthur Evans, the director of personnel, to sort out the offices from which we would work. Then Tony Byrne and I went to see Alfred Stocks, the chief executive. The first words I said to him were: "Alfie – stop the lot. Every single capital programme, everything you're doing. Don't sign for a penny until we've been through the books and decided how we're going to spend it."

Alfred Stocks is a wonderful bloke. As a chief executive he was superb. Until he retired in 1987 he had been in local government for forty years, and in Liverpool from 1973 had served eight different administrations.

He is a quiet little Yorkshireman and a perfect gent. His influence behind the scenes with Whitehall was immense. They held him in great esteem and often a quiet word from Alfie could persuade government officials to come north to Liverpool and look at the problems for themselves when otherwise they might not have bothered.

His experience and ability made many other chief executives look like office boys. People often used to ask him how on earth he managed to work with Derek Hatton. If they expected criticism they were disappointed. He once said: "Working with Derek has not been dull. It has been exciting from Day One and we have developed a good sparking relationship. No holds are barred and we are not frightened of each other. He does listen to me and in spite of any image people may have of him he does welcome advice."

He could be critical too of successive governments and the way they had starved Liverpool of much needed cash. He was once quoted as saying: "The city just cannot be expected to produce A1 services on C-minus funding."

I think he enjoyed working with us. At least from us he got decisions. We knew how to use the power we had been given. For years from the Liberals and Tories indecision had been the order of the day, and any local government officer will tell you that their lives are easier if they know what the policy is, and they know it is not going to change day by day. The Labour group had the majority. We could take decisions and know with impunity that they would be ratified by council meetings. It was a whole new ball game for Liverpool in terms of political control, and yes, some officers found it difficult to acclimatise themselves to it.

But even those individuals, who did not agree with what we were doing, were delighted on a professional level. The worst thing for an officer is to work for weeks on plans and proposals then have them thrown out at council meetings. Now at least they had the initiative of control.

The Militant philosophy was simple. For years we had controlled the District Labour Party, which was ultimately one of the accusations which cost me my membership of the Labour Party. Of course we controlled it. It was our power base. The only reason I am out in the political wilderness now is because we gave it away. But I'll say more about that later.

For the moment the reality was that even though we had taken power long before we ever anticipated, we had the machinery to guide us on our way. In Liverpool we had the people who could do the job. Backing us from London was the whole of Militant, who saw our victory as a major step forward.

The plan was quite straightforward. We had taken office. Now we would bring the train to a standstill. Everything had to stop. Then we would re-route the engine and the whole council train onto our track. Those who wanted to stay on board could do so, but anyone who objected to the route we were taking would have to go.

The way forward had been worked out five or six years earlier. We well knew what we wanted, and at the centre of it all was our Urban Regeneration Strategy: our plan for homes and houses. Some people have said it was an obsession with Tony Byrne and me. Maybe it was, but it was a magnificent obsession. Tony and I share one thing. We don't find politics very complicated. Politics is about life. Most people, whether they would articulate it this way or not, recognise that the two most important things to anyone are a job and a house. I know it is a contradiction in terms, but I would argue that most people, if they then had to choose between the two, would identify their home as the principal priority.

It seems so obvious what it must be like for a woman putting her kids to bed in a tenement where the walls are filthy and damp, where she's permanently worried about the security, the health and the well-being of her children. People cannot be happy like that – yet there are thousands in Liverpool who have had to survive in those conditions. The conclusions, in terms of a programme to rectify the situation, are self-evident. It took researchers at King's College, London, four and a half years of scientific study to produce a thesis on *Utopia on Trial* in 1985. Yet when we were visited by one of those involved, Professor Alice Coleman, she told us that we had reached the same conclusions on instinct.

National politicians make their judgements on a cost basis. Their objectives are wrong. The whole housing policy of this country has been flawed by the assumption that there is a crude surplus in housing, and all the disasters in public housing have been brought about as a consequence of that approach.

So we knew what we wanted, and we knew we were right. We were going to build 5,000 local authority houses, semi-detached and bungalows with gardens back and front, central heating, double glazing, and proper roads. Not high-rise buildings which end up derelict ten years later. We did that. We were pledged to create new jobs, and in the first year alone we took 1,000 youngsters off the dole and onto the council workforce through Manpower Service Commission schemes. But those jobs became more than just employment schemes – they became full-time posts. In addition in job terms we created 6,000 jobs in the private building sector as a result of our house-building programme.

It was all a part of our Urban Regeneration Strategy. We recognised that the physical squalor and deprivation of the inner city area and outer council estates was worsening. So we committed ourselves to tackling the problems of poor housing and environmental dereliction in which so many people had to live out their lives.

The main thrust of the plan was to select seventeen priority areas, where our proposals for improving the quality of life, with new houses, sports centres and environmental improvements, would affect the lives of 40,000 people.

And we got rid of the Lord Mayor – we weren't having any of that nonsense. The good old-fashioned position of chairman was what we wanted.

We knew we could carry the plan through because we had the people who could do the job. They have accused me of handing out jobs to the boys. Of course we did. We wanted people around us who understood the plan, who were committed to it. They criticised the public relations exercise, and said we had set up a Militant propaganda unit. So what's new in that? Of course we needed a propaganda unit. The world and his dog wanted to see us kicked in the teeth, and we would have been pretty naive not to protect ourselves.

Not everyone who went into that public relations machine were Militants when they began, but many are now. They saw what we stood for. They saw it working. They became politicised and understood it was the only way forward.

Where officials were concerned it was easy. If they accepted what we said, then that was fine. If they did not agree with what we said, but got on with their jobs, that was fine too. But I knew there were those who would try to undermine what we were doing. Like any organisation worth its salt who finds opponents in its ranks, we soon sorted them out. It was no witch-hunt as people claimed. It was common sense. We did not sack them – we shunted them sideways, and put them in positions where they could do least harm.

Some moaned and whined to the press. So what! I've never cared what people thought about me, but I cared that we should find the moles and move them, that we should find the leaks and stop them. Our campaign was more important than the careers of a few whingeing armchair radicals who hadn't the guts to stand up and be counted.

The Labour group itself presented fewer problems. In Militant we knew who were our allies. We knew where our strengths and weaknesses lay. We knew who we could and could not trust.

People like Tony Byrne and me adapted readily to the local government machine. We understood it, we could use it, and battle from inside it.

We had one odd thing in common. He had trained as a Jesuit priest. I had spent two years heavily involved with the Protestant Church, believing that something was wrong with the world and that perhaps religion could provide the answers. Neither of us got very far down that road, but now at least we shared a political faith.

From the word go, though we were as different as chalk and cheese, it was clear we were going to get on, and that we could work together. Over the years we have had our rows. Sometimes we almost came to blows, but there's never been an occasion where next day we were not battling together side by side. I suppose those kinds of disagreements are inevitable where two people are working so closely, with such intensity, and under such pressure.

He and I always knew that housing was the priority. In the Housing Sub-Committee of the District Labour Party it had been accepted without question that this was the case. In an area like Liverpool it could be no other way. If you were really going to do anything positive about changing conditions then you had to change the way that people lived. Had we all been social workers then we could have said "Let's provide new social services and pour millions into them." That would have been like treating cancer with a million aspirins. We had to start by removing the conditions which had created the cancer.

For Tony it was the one thing that mattered more than any other. He still lives to this day in the same little terraced house in which he was born, off Smithdown Road, Liverpool, complete with outside toilet.

There were others who were purely political animals – who formed the backbone of our thinking and policy-making – but who would never be great administrators. For instance, Tony Mulhearn. Tony had been a supporter of Militant long before I ever joined. There were few outside Militant headquarters in London who were a greater political influence on events than he was. But he simply did not adapt to the day-to-day running of the administrative machine, which is why for so long he stayed outside the Town Hall, first as vice-president and then as president of the District Labour Party.

To this day I still think it was a mistake to bring him onto the council. From his base within the DLP he was able to co-ordinate the strategy. When it came to keeping members of the Labour group in line if they faltered over policy decisions, it only took a few words from Tony to remind them that we were acting as a body, and not as individuals. On occasions like those he ruled with an iron hand behind the scenes but was always able to claim that he was distanced from us. Once he stood alongside us in the council chamber he became high profile, and was marked down as a target for Kinnock and the rest.

So in those early days it was the Hatton-Byrne duo which led the machine. That's not to say we could have done it without the Tony Mulhearns and the rest. People like Eddie Loyden, a former deputy leader of the Liverpool Labour group before he went off to Westminster as the MP for Liverpool Garston, and Ken Stewart, a former Labour housing chairman before he went off to the European Parliament as the MEP for Merseyside West, played an important part as well.

Then there was Hugh Dalton, who, apart from my personal admiration, I would describe as the greatest front figure, in the role of chairman, mayor or whatever, that any council could have. Whether he was chairing a rowdy council meeting and dealing with the Liberals under Sir Trevor Jones, whether he was entertaining a group of international businessmen and investors, or simply meeting ordinary folk for a pint in a pub in Scotland Road, Hughie could handle it.

Running a Town Hall is no different in principle from governing the country. It's just the scale of things which differs, and of course, you are working much closer to the grass roots. While Government has its departments, with ministers responsible for their own individual areas of concern, so local authorities have their committee structures – and the chairmen of those committees exercise considerable power.

In some cases they have delegated powers – and the ability to take decisions outside full meetings of the committees. The committees implement action in every area of the city's life, from social services to pub and club licences. But some are obviously more important than others. Finance, housing and education stand out for example as vital areas. So in May 1983 as we began to govern, selecting the right people to chair those committees was vital. We had overall control of the council, so we could do as we pleased. There was no way we were going to share anything with the Liberals. We wanted our own people in charge right across the board.

The chairmanship of Finance went to Tony Byrne. His grasp of economics was second to none, and he wasn't blinded by facts and figures. It was no good telling him there wasn't enough money in the budget to fulfil our promises. His attitude, like mine, was that the money would just have to be found. We would get on with the job and worry about the cash later.

One of our most controversial appointments was to give the post of Education chairman to twenty-four-year-old Dominic Brady. He was a first year Town and Country Planning student at the Liverpool Polytechnic who had left school at sixteen after taking his O levels. For a time he had worked as a school caretaker. But he was totally committed to our plans for the reorganisation of secondary education, in which we planned to have seventeen neighbourhood co-educational comprehensives – and of course, we had promised to keep open the Croxteth Comprehensive School. In his four years as a councillor for the Everton ward he had made education his specialist interest. Because he was young and relatively inexperienced the opposition and the press were out for his blood. How could a man with his background handle an important committee which had a budget of around £150 million at its disposal, they asked. But Dominic did a damned good job and proved them all wrong.

The other committee chairmanships were equally important. Heather Adams became chair of Social Services. She was and still is a probation officer and had been my agent back in 1978 when I first stood for the council. She is a quiet girl but with inner strengths, and was a caring and realistic chair of Social Services.

The chairmanship of the Housing Committee went in the first instance to an old stalwart, Ken Stewart, who had been shadow chairman for years when we were out of office. Later, when he left the council in June 1984 to become the European MP for Merseyside West, he was succeeded by Peter Owens who had been elected to the council on a Militant platform back in 1973.

A close friend of mine, Peter Lloyd – who was to be tragically killed in a holiday road accident in Spain in 1985 – became the chairman of Licensing and Marketing. He had been voted onto the council in 1978, and along with myself was part of the first Militant input. We were great mates. We had joined the Labour Party together, joined the council together and even went to the Everton matches together. His death was a great loss to the council. He was to be succeeded in a revamped Trading and Licensing Committee by an old friend and colleague of mine, John Nelson, a blunt, down-to-earth person who would stand no nonsense.

We made Tony Hood the chairman of the Planning Committee but he also played an important role as secretary of the

Labour group, which was later to involve him in negotiations with the Labour Party nationally when the threats of expulsion came along. He was a former community development officer and with his quiet air of authority was always a vital part of the delegations which would meet ministers and Labour party officials.

Chairman of the Leisure Committee was an ex-docker, Alex Doswell, secretary of the Liverpool Trades Council, and a very active member of the Transport and General Workers' Union. He has a long history of being in the Left minority against the old right-wing controlled Labour Party.

Paul Astbury, a plasterer by trade who was later to take over from me as deputy leader after the Militant expulsions, took the chairmanship of the Environmental Services Committee. He had emerged as a young councillor in the Childwall Valley area of the city where he had lived all his life, and was to go on to become another Militant supporter. His committee was responsible for everything from refuse collection to the care of the city's parks.

For myself I took the chairmanship of the Personnel Committee. We had decided on being elected that good relations with the trade unions and with the 31,000 council employees were vital. I had always been the shadow chairman of Personnel Services, and now I took over the running of the department, transforming it from the Personnel Committee into the Industrial and Public Relations Committee to strengthen the links with the trade unions through the Joint Shop Stewards Committee.

From 1981 onwards the Town Hall shop stewards had played an important part in the drive to get us into power and we had always said that once we were in office they would sit alongside us, and have their say in the running of the city. Now we delivered on our pledge.

They became an integral part of the decision-making process, a position they had never before achieved. They responded by throwing the weight of their numbers behind us, whether it was to produce 30,000 demonstrators on the streets or to pack out mass rallies and meetings. They were with us to a man at that stage. Their power base was built up to such an extent that their national and regional leaders had to bow to their opinions in Liverpool. They had swelled the effort on the doorsteps, canvassing in all the marginal wards for that 1983 election. Now they reaped their reward.

The one man on the outside from the start was John Hamilton, the leader of the group.

I say leader of the Labour group, but the truth is that for all those years as far as I was concerned John Hamilton was a nowhere man. The figurehead in the council chamber? No, Hugh Dalton was that. The figurehead when it came to decision-making and controversy? No, Derek Hatton was that. The figurehead on background policy? No, that was Tony Mulhearn. The figurehead to whom council officials referred on major financial matters? No, that was Tony Byrne.

With his old V-necked pullovers, his overcoat, battered trilby and specs, John always looked every inch the retired bachelor schoolmaster that he is. He often reminded me of Mr Magoo, the cartoon character, bumbling his way through life like a genial uncle. He has a long, long record of service in the Labour Party and first became leader of the Labour group in 1974 when his predecessor Bill Sefton retired.

John was on the soft left-wing of the party, a Quaker who was cast in the mould of old-style 1950s and 1960s Socialists. He was briefly toppled from his position as leader in 1978 in a coup led by right-winger Eddie Roderick. But he was voted back into power, largely at the instigation of the District Labour Party that same year. The DLP wanted the right wing stopped, and John was a popular choice, though to some extent he was a compromise candidate. There were those even then who would have preferred a leader from the hard Left.

By 1983 when we came to power though, the truth was that the Labour Party which John had supported in Liverpool was dead and buried. He was a man out of his time and there were calls to get rid of him and install someone from the hard Left in his place.

I saw him as a sad, misguided little man who desperately wanted to hang onto his title as leader of the Labour group. But he wouldn't harm a fly and we knew that it would be seen as inhumane if we removed a man who, in fairness, had given so many years of his life to the Labour Party.

So we let him stay as leader – and there he was on May 6th 1983, clutching his briefcase as he posed for the cameras, giving a victory wave outside the municipal buildings on the day that we took office.

Militant's view was quite clear. If we had got rid of him then it would have been seen as a clash of personalities, and not a political move. The political issues at stake were far too important to allow that to cloud matters. We knew that at no stage would the existence of John Hamilton prevent us doing our job. We knew too that he had his uses. The moderates who might feel inclined to rock the boat felt safe with John apparently in charge. If he voted for something it was good enough for them. We knew he would vote our way.

But I have to confess that John's continued leadership was one of the issues on which I differed with Militant. A good number of the influential Left argued from the moment that we were elected in 1983 that he should go. I tended to think that we should have got rid of him. I felt he was an albatross, and he came back to haunt us three years later when he denounced us. Tony Byrne shared that view. So did others. They thought he was ineffectual and a liability.

The only thing that can be said for him is that he stayed with us and faced up to bankruptcy and disqualification like the rest, but I could not have behaved as he did: one minute voting with us, and the next, voting against us.

I said all along that at some stage he would crack, and I was right. He sold out to Kinnock, and now he complains publicly about the way he was treated. What did he expect?

From the word go John appeared to toe the line, but behind the scenes I believed his behaviour was damaging to our cause. Instead of accepting that we should act in unison he took a very individualistic approach, and resented the fact that Militant was really shaping policy and leading the way. He could have been dangerous, but we knew how to deal with him. We simply isolated him. His office was down the corridor from mine, and though initially we tried to involve him in the decision-making process he was having none of it. He wanted to lead the machine but didn't want to be part of it. We wanted to speak with one voice. What kind of a leader was he supposed to be?

So we let him go his own sweet way, but made sure that we kept a careful eye on him. He became a sad old figure who had put his whole life into the Labour and trade union movement, but at the end allowed himself to be swayed by people, like Kinnock, who are supposed to be fighting the Government.

At the height of the Militant witch-hunt I was often asked if prior to council and committee meetings in Liverpool we got together to organise our strategy and tactics. Very often I just said "No". What I was really saying was: "Mind your own business."

But of course it was a fact that before meetings of the District Labour Party, before trade union meetings, before council policy meetings, Militant supporters always gathered to discuss our plans. Sometimes we met alone – sometimes with others on the hard Left, though not necessarily within Militant. The final decisions were taken at open, democratic meetings, whether it was inside a trade union or inside the Labour Party: but because we were so well organised those decisions would always have our stamp on them.

Not that this strategy is unique to Militant. Groups like Tribune and Solidarity have always staged pre-emptive meetings in this way. What rankled with the opposition was that we succeeded where they failed. We kept our mouths shut and got on with the job – leaving the press and the right wing to accuse us of plotting behind everyone's backs. The loyalty and solidarity of Militants is second to none.

I was also frequently asked over the three years in office whether Militant, from its London base, helped determine the policy and tactics in Liverpool. Again I said: "It's none of our concern."

Now, as a leading Militant figure, I am able to say that the influence of, and input from, Militant's headquarters in London was immense. There is no getting away from the fact that the battles and campaigns being waged in Liverpool embodied Militant's aims and objectives nationally. Indeed in *Militant* as a paper the reports of our successes on Merseyside were evidence for the movement as a whole that our aims and objectives were coming to fruition.

We were the first group of Militants to experience real political power, and were therefore moving into unknown territory. It would have been unthinkable that the political minds and brains concentrated in London should not be tapped to help us chart our course. Not just through the thoughts expressed in *Militant* as a paper, but through meetings, discussions and phone calls.

One person, though, stands head and shoulders above the rest in helping orchestrate our campaign. Peter Taaffe, the man at the helm of Militant, is, as I conceded earlier, my foremost political influence. What's more, as someone born on Merseyside, he had first-hand knowledge of the problems which Liverpool faced, and had a natural affinity with our cause which others might not have been able to demonstrate.

I have never known such a clear thinker, or such a tactical genius. Politics is not about building up the individual, but within any Socialist struggle individuals do emerge. Where the development of Militant and its ideals is concerned that individual is Peter Taaffe. Since we first met back in the 1970s he has been my sounding board. It also must be said that the long-standing inspirational figure of Trotskyism in Britain, Ted Grant, the founder of Militant in Britain, was a significant influence at all times.

That doesn't mean we got hold of Peter Taaffe and took him to every District Labour Party meeting to tell people how to vote. In fact I can't remember that he's ever been to a DLP meeting in the city in his life, but certainly I would telephone him for advice and guidance, and take his ideas back to the Militant planning meetings. His lessons in how to organise within the Labour and trade union movements were invaluable, and we put them to good use.

SIX

LIVERPOOL VERSUS LONDON

I have sometimes been accused, even by my own friends in Militant, of playing the personality game: of allowing Derek Hatton to get in the way of the message.

The truth is that in the battle for Liverpool's survival we needed to use every trick in the book, and to face up to the national political figures ranged against us, we had to employ the same tactics.

Whether it was against Thatcher, Kinnock, Patrick Jenkin or Kenneth Baker, people thought twice about taking me on. They certainly knew that if they tried they would get as good as they gave.

I've always had a simple philosophy about Whitehall politicians who I sometimes believe think they are God. Whenever I'm seated across the table from them, I just look at them and think: "You've got two eyes, two ears, a nose and a mouth. So have I. Now let's see how good you are." It might sound arrogant, but it is true. What's more it works. In those three and a half years I met some of the most powerful people in Britain, and I can't say I was intimidated by a single one.

I made myself many enemies in high places, and the pressure I was under at that time, in the middle of 1983, was intense. I doubt I would have got through it, had it not been for the fact that back at home were Shirley and the children. They were my constant touchstone, and enabled me to keep my feet firmly on the ground.

One of the drawbacks I faced increasingly at that time in the middle of 1983 was that of being recognised wherever I went. So my home, with my Shirley, Rebecca, Ben, Sarah and Laura, was the place where I really switched off. Not that it was always easy. Being a Liverpool councillor meant that you were living on the job, and there were constantly people on the phone or knocking at the door.

In the quiet moments I simply like to laze around, and I tended not to arrive home and start talking to Shirley about the political scene. I lived that every moment of my life, and it was essential sometimes to get away from it. My idea of heaven is to put my feet up and watch any of the old Hollywood movies, many of which I have on tape. I adore Humphrey Bogart and Ingrid Bergman, and the copy of *Casablanca* I have on video has been run so many times it's a wonder it's not worn out.

However, with four active youngsters in the house, it's not often that I'm left with time on my hands. Becky, the eldest, has her mother's passion for horse riding, and spends every minute of her spare time at the stables. She has developed into a very good little rider, and has taken several firsts at local shows. Sarah too loves riding, but she also shares my passion for sport, and is heavily involved with gymnastics. Ben is very much his father's son, and is such a promising footballer that he has already won a place in the Liverpool schoolboys' side. Laura is the baby of the family, but already is showing every sign that she will be as active as the others.

They are a fantastic set of kids, and they have very wise heads for their ages. They have managed to cope so well under all the pressure that has gone with my job, and, as you might imagine, they have a healthy disregard for the press and a rooted distrust of all reporters and photographers.

When we go on holiday as a family – and, as an escape, we always try to go abroad – Shirley and I love to take our own apartment or villa with the children so that we can relax. It is the one time when I can laze around and do nothing. The rest of the time I suppose I live my life in the fast lane, at quite a ferocious pace; a holiday to me is simply lying in the sun from morning till night and getting up only to go to the bar, the beach or a restaurant. I'm certainly not a great one for sightseeing.

As for Shirley, she shares my political views, though clearly she is not as involved with the world of politics as I am, especially since the children came along.

'Though I have never been simply Mrs Derek Hatton, but Shirley Hatton in my own right, I knew when to step out of the limelight.

That doesn't mean I've stayed in the background in every area of Derek's life. I certainly didn't politically. From the days when I pushed Rebecca round in her pram canvassing for votes in Derek's first election campaign, to the part I played in the Labour Party locally, I've scarcely been a shrinking violet. Indeed I was one of those who helped set up the Women's Council locally within the Labour Party.

What I did was to step back at the right time. As Derek became more and more a national figure, and a target for certain elements within the media, I simply moved myself out of the public eye, though I was still involved in everything he was doing.

Our home life was the most important thing to me. We never really talked about having children, though when people look at the family, with a two-year gap between each of the first three, and then three years before the final child, they assume we must have planned it all very carefully. Not a bit of it. They just happened like that.

Considering that Derek had been an only child he turned out to be the perfect father. He was always there to change the nappies,

75

*never once complained and seemed to love every minute of it. He
was like that with Becky, and as Ben came along – then Sarah and
Laura – he never changed. He was never one to expect the woman
in his life to take care of it.*

*In fact I can't think of any other man in our entire group of
friends who was as much involved as a father when his children
were small, and it's a closeness which has continued across the
years as they have grown. In the real sense of the word he enjoys
his children, and will always make time for them. At weekends
they run rings round him. One is dancing, one is playing football,
another wants to go out to the stables. He never grows tired of it or
tries to put the onus on me.*

*Mind you, from 1983 onwards, after Labour had taken over at
the Town Hall, the pressure at home was considerable. There were
always people ringing up, or calling round. During those early
months after taking power, Derek seemed to spend most of his time
having discussions about money – or rather the shortage of it. If I
had ever thought that balancing the household budget was a tricky
job, it seemed as nothing compared with the problems of balancing
the Town Hall budget.'*

When we came to power that May, in 1983, the simple truth
was that the city just didn't have enough money. From 1979,
when Thatcher was voted into Downing Street, Liverpool had
suffered under the Tory cuts. Councils had been told to get
spending down, and Liverpool had been faced with demands to
reduce spending by £300 million. By 1980 Michael Heseltine,
the then Environment Secretary, was cutting rate support
grants, and Liverpool stood to lose £3.4 million.

By 1981 it was calculated that the city would end the
year £36 million in the red if it didn't meet the Government's
spending limits. By the end of 1982 the Liberals were talking
about rate rises of up to 30 per cent to solve the crisis – and
Heseltine slashed one per cent off the following year's budget
for overspending.

By March 1983 the situation was even worse. The Liberals
budgeted for £219 million to run the city. But the Government

said that budget must be trimmed to £212 million. The Liberals brought in a rate increase of only seven per cent hoping it would be a vote-winner – but even that tactic failed to save them at the polls. So when we came to power, we were operating with a Liberal budget which was already in excess of the £212 million which was the target figure with which we were supposed to work.

There was no way that we could carry through our planned programme of house-building and the Urban Regeneration Strategy on that kind of budget without cuts. But our election slogan was: "No cuts in jobs and services". The stage was set for our financial battle with Whitehall. As far as we were concerned the Government had stolen £120 million from Liverpool by cuts in rate support grants, and the changes they had made in the way local councils were funded. We simply wanted £30 million back.

We were running the city on the Liberals' budget, but we were not prepared to bring in massive rate increases to solve the crisis. Our spending plans meant that we were heading for a budget deficit of £25 million. But we told Whitehall that if they wanted cuts they would have to come and do it themselves. They responded by singling us out as the bad boys in the overspending league. So began our campaign to make the Government foot the bill.

By this time Michael Heseltine had been replaced as Environment Secretary, and the man holding the local government purse strings was Patrick Jenkin.

I felt he was completely out of his depth and was simply being used by the Government. He was an old-fashioned Tory, who didn't see the fight with Liverpool as a class battle, and in fact, as long as the Tory system could be maintained, didn't want a battle at all. Those around him did, so he was under pressure from all sides, from his own colleagues, the Cabinet, the civil servants, and, in Liverpool, from the likes of Derek Hatton.

My view is that he simply did not know how to handle us. When Tony Byrne and I went to his offices at the Department of the Environment, we would deliberately play a mischievous double act. We ran rings round him. One of us would play Mr Nice and the other Mr Nasty. Then we would suddenly change roles. Very few people have been able to cope with that combination.

We meant to get the money from Jenkin. What's more we didn't ask for it, or look for it first. If you hold back until you have the cash, nothing gets done. If you go out and give out the contracts, start buying the materials, add to the payroll, and then look round for the money, it's one hell of an incentive for finding it.

Whenever we met Jenkin he was flanked by a team of civil servants, who would spend their time whispering advice, and passing notes to him. The problem with Patrick Jenkin was that I don't think he understood the complexities of the issue. He certainly didn't understand the total politics of it – that as Labour councillors from the hard Left there could be no compromise on our part with a Tory Government. We had made our promises to the people who elected us. We meant to keep them no matter what the price.

We weren't being irresponsible, as people have claimed. I don't think it is possible to work in local government yet not accept that you have to manage the resources which are available to you. There is a difference between that, and accepting constraints placed upon you.

As the months went by in 1983 the financial crisis deepened. By the autumn Patrick Jenkin was warning that we might face suspension and legal action if we didn't toe the line and balance the books. They said we were heading for bankruptcy, and there were plans to send in government commissars to run the city. What a bluff! Even if they had managed to get into the Town Hall, did they really think anyone was going to help them?

Then, as a Christmas present, Jenkin announced council spending limits for 1984. We were told our new target for the next financial year would be £216 million – three million pounds less than the Liberals had said they needed to run the city in 1983! It was a nonsense and proved how iniquitous was the Tory strategy of imposing spending limits.

In February 1984 Tony Byrne, John Hamilton and myself went to London to tell Jenkin that we wanted back the £30 million the Tories had stolen. That would allow us to balance our budget for the following year. But he flatly refused, and told us we would be breaking the law if we went ahead and planned to spend more money than we had.

You would have thought that we would have had the backing of Kinnock and the Labour Party nationally in our fight. Not so. We went to a Labour Party conference on local government that month, and they refused to back us. Kinnock was clearly worried sick that he would damage his standing in the country if he was seen to be prepared to break the law. He didn't even come to Liverpool to see for himself.

The same was true of the trendies and hooray Henries from the London boroughs. They just didn't understand how bad things were in Liverpool, nor the level of commitment. So we were out on our own.

Budget Day was set for March 29th, 1984. To keep our promises to the people who elected us, we were committed to spending that £30 million no matter what.

We were, of course, also in the run-up to the local elections again, and it was vital that we should keep control of the city and strengthen our hand. The conflict between ourselves and the Government now amounted to an all-out battle, as we laid our plans for Budget Day.

The headlines came and went. "City in Crisis". "Bankruptcy faces Liverpool". All the time the groundswell was building up against Jenkin as we orchestrated the campaign against the Government to persuade them to give us more money. We organised marches, rallies and demonstrations. The media had used me, now I used them.

Budget Day was March 29th, 1984, but ten days before the meeting came the first official warning that our necks were on the block if we went ahead with an illegal budget, ignoring spending limits, and not increasing rates enough to bring in the necessary cash.

Every town council has a district auditor who is almost an extension of the local treasury department. Not only is he effectively the "public watchdog", checking that councillors stay within the law on spending, but he also offers advice and guidance. Until 1985 our district auditor was a man called Les Stanford, with whom we had a very close relationship. We met him regularly. In fact the meetings became so frequent that it became a joking matter that we were off to see the district auditor again. We would go in with the chief executive, Alfred Stocks, and the treasurer, Mike Reddington. Once Tony Byrne and I had explained our outline plans, we would leave the officers to get on with the discussion.

Stanford knew our political position, and that was never debated. What he wanted was the detail, and we felt it important that he should be involved, and understand what our aims and objectives were. He was even invited along when we held exhibitions and displays to spell out our urban strategy. So in no sense was he seen as an enemy of the city, but rather as an ally.

But now it was clear the knives were being sharpened, because on March 19th, 1984 he sent every councillor a letter warning of the consequences of an illegal budget.

He told us: "The council is elected to carry out its programme and functions within the law. So long as it does so lawfully neither I nor the courts will question the substance of what it decides. Where, however, it comes to my notice that serious breaches of the law may be contemplated I have a responsibility to report them in the public interest. In my opinion the council would clearly be in breach of its legal duty if, in the event, it failed to make an adequate rate."

What's more he went on to say there would be serious consequences for councillors and council employees, as levying an inadequate rate would lead to the money running out, and, in law, we wouldn't be able to make good that shortfall by borrowing.

He said: "There will in short be a serious breakdown. The making of an inadequate rate would inevitably result in losses to the council and it would be my clear and unavoidable duty to consider whether those losses should be recovered."

Stanford spelt out to each of us in that letter that councillors would be personally liable to make good any financial loss – and could face disqualification from office if the amount involved was more than £2,000. The deliberate making of such a rate, he said, was likely to be taken as wilful misconduct on our part.

The majority of the Labour group took it all as just another scare tactic inspired by Patrick Jenkin. But the letter was enough to scare the living daylights out of six councillors on the right wing, led by fifty-five-year-old shopkeeper, Eddie Roderick, the man who had tried and failed to stage a take-over of the leadership years earlier.

The half-a-dozen so-called moderates staged a rebellion. We had put forward proposals for a budget of £245 million, leaving us short of almost £30 million. We insisted this should come from Whitehall. The six rebels announced publicly that they would defy the Whip and would not back an illegal budget.

The trouble was that without the votes of the rebels who we called the Scabby Six, we knew we could not get that budget through. They had gone with us all the way and shared the glory of success and achievements from the moment we were elected in 1983. Their votes were vital, but they hadn't the guts to stay in there and fight when the chips were down.

Publicly we boasted that we would still carry the day, and behind the scenes we worked with the council trade unions to orchestrate a massive demonstration on Budget Day. Over 25,000 people massed outside the Town Hall in Castle Street that afternoon. I told the six rebels that they might go in and vote against us, but they would have to come out and face the wrath of the crowd outside.

Privately though we knew it was a no-win situation. So before the budget meeting we sat down to plan an alternative strategy, though we knew we were being forced down a road we would not have chosen. The only thing we could now engineer was to make no decision and leave our policy intact.

The meeting went on for eight hours and was pure farce. Our so-called illegal budget, calling for a nine per cent rate rise, was on the table, but the six traitors defected. They produced an amendment suggesting that the budget process be postponed till April 11th to allow council officials to prepare a "legal" budget. But as Budget Day was the last working day of the financial year, that meant no one in the council offices was authorised to approve the payment of bills, and in theory the running of the city would come to a standstill.

We saw our chance to cut the ground from under the feet of the rebels and the Liberals. We added a rider to the motion that I along with our so-called leader John Hamilton and finance chairman Tony Byrne should, in the interim, form an emergency committee to control the city's finances. The rebels backed that move thinking we had seen sense. The Tories too went with it, seeing it as the only way of making progress. The Liberals, we knew, would oppose it, because they were not going to have any say on the emergency committee.

Had we then voted with the rebels and the Tories the plan would have gone through. We didn't. We abstained. The result: the six scabs and the eighteen Tories voted together for our emergency committee plan. The Liberals voted against it. But because we didn't vote at all the plan was defeated – no decision at all was taken – and the meeting ended in chaos with no rate having been set at all.

On April 25th, there was another budget meeting. Only five of the six deserters were there, and again they voted against our proposals. The Liberals and the Tories were in disarray and could not agree on an alternative. So once again the council meeting ended in chaos with no decision made – and once again no rate was set.

Our plan now was to postpone any decisions on new rates and the budget until after May 3rd, 1984. That, of course, was the day of the local elections. If we could stave off the attacks till then, and avert the looming financial crisis, we could fight

Above. Here's me, aged about 18 months, with Mam behind the Police Training Centre in Mather Avenue where my grandad was a mounted policeman.

Right. This is the first big fight I ever won – the Butlins Cup for Schoolboy Boxing, at Pwllheli, North Wales, when I was about 8.

Below. Posing for my first official photo, aged 5, at Rudston Road Primary School, Liverpool.

Above. Number 162 shows off his muscles, at Butlins again.

Left. My wedding to Shirley, 29th August 1970, at All Saints Church, Childwall, with Shirley's sister Pam (holding my cousin Wendy), best man Phil Woods and guest of honour Flash the dog.

Below. In 1966, fed up with office work, I decided to follow my Dad into the fire service. This is an early hot encounter while training in Speke.

Previous page:
Top. At the Meccano factory demo, 1980.

Middle left. Addressing a rally in Liverpool, watched by Tony Mulhearn (far left). MP Eddie Loyden (with the hat) and Ian Lowes (second from right).

Middle right. In fighting spirit with MP Eric Heffer (back left) and Bob Parry and Bob Waring on the right.

Bottom left. With Patrick Jenkin (centre) on a visit to Everton to look at housing projects. Euro MP Ken Stewart is on the left and Tony Byrne on the right.

Bottom right. Talking to Tony Benn during the one-day strike in September 1985, with council leader John Hamilton (left), Bob Waring (centre) and Tony Mulhearn (right).

This page:
Top. Campaigning outside the Town Hall with John Hamilton and Tony Mulhearn.

Right. Sitting on my controversial car.

Above. With Tony Mulhearn after the NEC inquiry into the District Labour Party, January 1986.

Above. Congratulating Felicity Dowling after her victory in Speke in the council elections, May 1986.

Above. Press conference on my resignation as deputy leader of the council, 25th November 1986.

At the head of the anti-government demonstration during the one-day strike, September 1985.

Above. In serious mood at the Old Swan by-election in Liverpool.

Below. Relaxing on holiday on the Costa del Sol, summer 1986, with Shirley and the kids (from left to right – Sarah, Laura and Rebecca).

Outside the Town Hall in Liverpool 1987.

for backing at the polls, and give two fingers to the opposition.

We stalled for time as the pressure mounted. Patrick Jenkin exhorted us to borrow money and set a rate of 60 per cent. The threats to bring in government commissioners to run the Town Hall were repeated, and Jenkin warned again that if we maintained our stance then we might face disqualification and surcharge for failing to set a legal rate. The vultures were hovering.

The longer we stalled, the louder we shouted about the missing money which the Government had taken and the nearer we went to the brink, the greater the pressure on Patrick Jenkin to find some sort of a settlement.

The word began to come back from London that if we met him again, and were prepared to compromise, perhaps some money might be available from inner city partnership funds.

What clinched it, and really strengthened our hand, were the May election results. If ever there was proof that people believed in what we were doing, it was the landslide win which gave us an overall majority of seventeen seats. The Liberals lost two seats, the Tories five, and we increased our grip by seven seats. Now the votes of the six rebels didn't count at all. There was going to be no stopping us.

Jenkin tried to bluff by issuing a statement saying that elections could not change the law, and that we had a legal duty to make a budget and set a rate.

We were due to hold another budget meeting on May 15th, 1984 but then the news was leaked that Jenkin planned to fulfil an earlier promise to come to Liverpool. He had played right into our hands! We postponed the meeting. Try as he might when he then arrived in the city on June 7th 1984 to claim he was only there to look at housing conditions, everyone assumed that he was also there to discuss Liverpool's finances. It was a propaganda victory as far as we were concerned, and Jenkin helped our case when he conceded: "I have seen some families living in conditions the like of which I have never seen before."

83

If that wasn't a boost for our demands to have more money for housing I don't know what was.

And in addition, in the weeks of negotiation with Whitehall which followed, even Jenkin's own civil servants admitted that Liverpool could not balance its budget without a massive rates increase.

Our case was also helped by the fact that all the forecasts that we would run out of money and the city would come to a standstill proved to be a nonsense. It was business as usual.

Against the background of the miners' strike Jenkin finally gave in to another meeting. The Government were fighting Arthur Scargill on one front. They didn't want a second front with Derek Hatton, Militant and all that entailed. Jenkin was under pressure to find a solution.

Tony Byrne, Tony Mulhearn, John Hamilton and I travelled down on the train to London on July 9th, 1984. When we got to the Department of the Environment Jenkin was obviously on the spot. Finally he delivered the goods, a package wrapped up to preserve credibility, as money he had "found" through partnership schemes. After all the talk about "There's no question of giving Liverpool more money – there just isn't any," here he was saying he'd suddenly found some.

Now he had to present the deal without loss of face and had in mind a simultaneous announcement by his department and ourselves so that we couldn't grab the glory. He must have been naive to think we would wait until the next day.

We kept our part of the bargain till we got home. We said nothing to the press waiting outside his London office except that there had been "very fruitful talks". Fruitful! Me using the language of the Tory press office. But back in Liverpool our people were waiting. They wanted a victory. We were about to give it to them. So we kept quiet for just as long as it took that intercity train to pull into Lime Street Station. Then we made straight for the municipal buildings and shouted the news from the roof-tops.

We had won! The Government had capitulated. This was what Labour could do in Liverpool! I'll never forget the scene outside our offices. There were TV lights and cameras, and a huge crowd of our supporters cheering and singing.

Two days later we held the much-postponed budget meeting. We calculated that in our back pockets we now had concessions from Jenkin by way of grants and other aid which, with promises that he had made for future assistance, were worth over £50 million. We were able to go ahead and set a "legal" budget, with a rate increase of seventeen per cent.

Jenkin was furious. He believed, in his own words, that we had "danced on his political grave" and Liverpool became his personal *bête noire*. The defeat cost him his job, of course. Later that year they brought in Kenneth Baker. It is true though that the episode soured our relations with Whitehall from that day on. Jenkin vowed to deal with every single matter relating to Liverpool personally – even the smallest of details. Derek Hatton had rubbed his face in the muck, and he wasn't going to forget it.

It was all summed up at the time by Tory MP Teddy Taylor. I met him one evening when I travelled up to Glasgow, to appear on Scottish Television soon after winning our battle in Liverpool for more money. Taylor was on the same programme, and afterwards, in the hospitality room, couldn't resist having a go at me, especially as I was with Bob Wylie, the Militant organiser for Scotland. "You do realise," he said, "that we had to tell Patrick to give you the money. At this stage we want Scargill. He's our priority. But we'll come for you later."

To the best of my recollection these were the words he used, and how true they turned out to be. They did want Scargill, and they did come for us later.

S E V E N

THE NET CLOSES

All through our year-long battle with Patrick Jenkin the one person who was conspicuous by her absence was Margaret Thatcher. She must have known the sort of reception she would get, and we didn't disappoint her when she finally came to Liverpool. It is one of my abiding memories: the day we made the prime minister bend over.

She had picked her day well, right in the middle of the Labour Party conference in Blackpool in October 1984. Her advisers had obviously told her that if she went to Liverpool then she would be guaranteed plenty of publicity, but the Hattons of this world would be out of the way.

The news leaked out, and we rang from the conference to ask if she would sit down and talk with us. There were no letters, no formal invitations. The situation just developed, but once she was in Liverpool we knew she would find it difficult not at least to meet us informally.

The meeting was arranged late in the afternoon, in the Manpower Services Commission's offices in the centre of Liverpool. There were five of us from the Labour group: myself, Tony Byrne, John Hamilton, Tony Hood and Frank Mills. Alongside us were the chief executive Alfred Stocks, and the city treasurer, Mike Reddington. We sat and waited as the clock ticked round, and it was the waiting which was finally her downfall.

I hate being kept hanging round by anyone, no matter who they are. So I said to Tony Byrne: "What we need here is a tactical advantage. Otherwise she's going to come walking in, with her massive entourage, as the caring prime minister visiting little old Liverpool, and she'll have the psychological advantage of finding us sitting here like lemons. What we have to do is switch the roles."

Mind you we had already planned to embarrass her. Each of us had propped in front of us on the large table a piece of card, which had "£30 million" written on it. It wasn't exactly a subtle way of reminding her of the money the Government had stolen from the city, but we couldn't resist the gesture.

Now I came up with something else. "When she walks in she's going to expect us to shake hands," I told Tony Byrne. "It would be petty if we didn't, but if we don't stand up, she'll have to lean across the table and bend over to shake hands with each of us."

Tony Byrne loved the idea, and the others joined in. Not Alfred Stocks, and Mike Reddington, of course. They were far too much the diplomats as council officers to be involved in anything like that. In any case, it didn't matter. They were going to be the last to shake hands.

It worked like a treat. In she breezed, and couldn't believe her eyes when we all sat there without moving.

She stood in front of John Hamilton and me, and then had to bend over and reach across this huge table to grasp us by the hand. Each of the hangers on, including, of all people, poor old Patrick Jenkin, then had to follow suit. She was livid. You could sense throughout the meeting that she was furious, but it put us on top and we stayed there.

We won every argument, and then, just as she was standing up to leave, I sprang another move she was not expecting. The meeting came just at the time when thirty-seven men who had occupied an oil rig at the Cammell Laird shipyard in Birkenhead – in protest over redundancies – had been arrested and taken off to Liverpool's Walton Jail. I said to her: "By the way, before you go, there are thirty-seven lads who are stuck in jail because of your attitude over Cammell Laird's. What are you going to do about it?"

It was completely out of the blue and she was furious. I remember it so well. "As far as I'm concerned Mr Hatton," she snorted, "if I'd had any respect for you before today – which I don't think I had – then it would certainly have gone by now." That was her parting shot, and she stormed out.

Having said all that, I only wish the Labour Party nationally had someone who could represent the working class as a leader in the way she represents the Tory class. The ruling classes – the owners and controllers of business in this country – put Thatcher into power, and gave her the leadership of the party. She has represented their interests to the letter, and has gone right down the line politically and tactically.

I'm not saying I respect the person, but I do respect her loyalty to the people who put her where she is, and the way in which she has publicly demonstrated that loyalty.

If the Labour leadership had approached the principles of Socialism with the vigorous, forthright and determined attitude with which she has approached the principle of capitalism, we would have won the 1983 election by a mile.

It's in stark contrast with the lack of respect Neil Kinnock shows for those who made him leader of the Labour Party. But the party conference that autumn in 1984, when Thatcher made her visit, should have proved to him once and for all that Liverpool's example in taking on the Tories was one he would do well to follow.

We went to that conference as heroes. We had defeated Patrick Jenkin and kept our promises to the Labour voters. Houses were being built. The city was being transformed. Now we wanted the Labour Party to come out and do what they had so far refused to do – publicly support us. We moved a resolution of support for any local authority who took on the campaign for more resources even if it meant breaking the law.

Eric Heffer, one of our own MPs from Liverpool, was the chairman. He had always backed us, and allowed a procession of Liverpool speakers to take the rostrum. The atmosphere was tremendous. Every time someone from Merseyside got up to speak, there were resounding cheers. Kinnock looked grim. He saw us as an electoral liability, and had made it clear that there was no way he would be a party to sanctioning councils like Liverpool in breaking the law. He and others, including John Cunningham, the Labour spokesman on local government, had argued that the battle against rate-capping, the new measure planned by the Tories to impose limits on high-spending Labour councils, was paramount. They took the view that urging people to break the law would damage Labour's image with the electorate.

They argued that we had no alternative but to increase rates to meet the gap in the budget. It was a despicable attitude, but at least it was to prove consistent. They were against us then, and they have been against us ever since. In my view Kinnock's attitude typified the new trendy – later to become "yuppie" – style of Labour Party politics, which held sway in the South. They were more concerned with image than with reality. The London boroughs with their obsessions about anti-racist and anti-sexist issues were classic examples, but even Manchester, Sheffield and other Labour councils across the country could sometimes display the same attributes. So it wasn't so much a North-South geographical divide. It was really a gulf between areas like Merseyside which had strong working-class traditions, and councillors whose roots were in the towns and cities they represented, and boroughs where the new middle classes predominated.

Talking at that conference to members of the Labour Party from those kinds of places it was clear we were miles apart. They couldn't cope with us, because what we said, we did. They could never be like us, and though I am sure they secretly envied us, they would never admit it.

Those differences had been evident throughout 1984 as we joined up with those other Labour councils to unite in the battle against government cuts in local authority spending. Councils like Islington and Sheffield saw themselves as rebels cast in the same mould as Liverpool. But when it came to the crunch they just didn't have our bottle.

We were hatching our budget plans for 1985 – plans which again required more money from the Government. It had all the makings of a re-run of the battle with Patrick Jenkin, but this time it was a different ball game. Now the Tories were determined to stand their ground. The other councils were also in confrontation, so under the auspices of the Local Government Information Unit we were meeting that autumn to plan our joint tactics. It was at that stage that the ill-fated decision to postpone setting a rate in 1985 – the decision which was to lead to disqualification – was taken.

Councils like Sheffield and Islington argued that the issue we should all take back to our towns and cities was that of rate-capping, and that we should campaign on the streets against it. Our approach was much more direct. "People won't understand that kind of campaign against Thatcher," we told them time and again. "But they will understand a campaign which says: give us back the money you are stealing, otherwise it will cost jobs, and will damage services."

We battled constantly too against the tactic of refusing to set rates unless the Government produced more money. It was a totally negative strategy. "How can you motivate people into supporting you by sitting back and doing nothing?" we said. They wouldn't be swayed, and, on the basis of one for all and all for one, we went with them.

The people I really despised were politicians like David Blunkett, the leader of Sheffield City Council. I believe that he and others must have known that when it came to the crunch they would never be able to carry with them their individual Labour groups back home on a policy of breaking the law and refusing to set a rate. Yet they sat in those meetings in London, behaving like middle class intellectuals – the true "loony left". It was the typical London borough approach to politics. They appeared more concerned that we called the chairman the chairperson or a manhole cover a personhole cover, than they ever were about the real issues.

I remember two blazing rows with women from London. On one occasion I flew at Margaret Hodge, the leader of Islington Council, and told her, "If you don't like the heat you should get out of the kitchen." Immediately another woman councillor ripped into me and accused me of being sexist because I had mentioned a woman and the kitchen in the same breath!

On another occasion they had spent hours discussing who should be on the platform for a national public rally, and just when we had sorted it out, up they popped to demand equal numbers of men and women. I lost my rag, turned to John Hamilton and said: "Hey John, if you put a skirt on that should solve the problem!" You can imagine the sort of reaction that aroused!

Those meetings were unbelievable. Backing us from Liverpool we had thousands of working people committed to a cause. The rest of the council leaders, with honourable exceptions, sat there operating in isolation, playing bluff to see how long they could stay in the game before their own parties pulled the plugs.

They were simply trying to save face by hanging on till the last minute, when they had known all along they could not deliver the goods.

It was like having a palsy which got progressively worse. Disaster was inevitable.

We had known all along that we were being forced down the wrong road. Only weeks earlier, when we came back from meeting the other Labour councils, having agreed against our better judgement to the "do-nothing" policy, another Militant councillor, Felicity Dowling, had gone berserk and rightly warned me of the consequences. She had spent months, she said, arguing publicly against a no-rates stand, yet we had come back and adopted it.

We were trapped into a philosophy with which not only were we at odds as individuals, but one which our own District Labour Party saw as a "negative, do-nothing" position. They saw it as a dangerous piece of brinkmanship which would only blunt the hard campaigning edge and demanding voice of the city.

Our reasoning was simple. Had we refused to join the rest, Liverpool would have been isolated and we might have been seen as the only Labour council not to join the fight. We were trapped by the traditions of the Labour movement which say you have to follow the majority decision, and we were torn as leaders between the immediate outcome and what we privately knew were the inevitable consequences. We would be labelled mavericks.

At the end of the day we believed we would be isolated anyway, as the only Labour council left in the fight. So it proved. The battle was lost before it began.

With hindsight perhaps we should have gone it alone again that year, and not joined the discussions with the other Labour councils. Had we campaigned on our own, whether we had won or lost, the others would not have been embarrased by our stand. Perhaps the vicious backlash we ultimately suffered might have been softened.

Worse than that, Tony Byrne and I always knew in our hearts that the other authorities would drop out – and sure enough, one by one they did except for Lambeth who went on to make such a brave and magnificent stand.

While all the discussions about the fight against the Government went on, back at the Town Hall in Liverpool that November 1984, we faced a continuing budget crisis. Patrick Jenkin had promised as part of his package to give us £130 million towards our house building programme for 1985–86. Now he reneged on his promise. We met his civil servants on

November 5th, 1984 to spell out our strategy – but they denied that any such promise had been made.

On November 28th, 1984 Kenneth Baker, who had taken over as Minister for Housing and Local Government under Jenkin in the Department of the Environment, issued a statement in which he claimed we were living "in cloud cuckoo-land". But he wasn't having a go at Liverpool. He was attacking Militant. He said: "It is clearer than ever that responsibility is not a word which the Militant Tendency understand.

"The council are once again claiming that a strategy of high spending with no rent or rate increases is the only way to save jobs and maintain services. They were wrong about this in the summer. They are wrong now. It is a cruel deception."

Baker repeated the lie that Jenkin had not promised us the £130 million and went on to say: "The council should have learnt that this Government does not yield to blackmail. They threaten chaos and hope we will respond with extra money. They gained nothing by their antics in the summer and they will gain nothing by a repeat performance. The council should understand this now. They know what must be done to rein back spending, to reduce costs and to improve the efficiency of their services. They must do it and do it on their own."

Baker was clearly still reacting to the bloody nose we had given Jenkin in the previous summer. But there was more. We had already been told that our spending target for 1985 was to be £222 million, only £6 million more than in 1984. Now that they were refusing us the £130 million they had promised, and with our own budget for the next year set at £265 million, we were on course for yet another head-on confrontation with Whitehall.

The position became even worse in December when the Government announced national housing programme cuts which slashed even more cash from our funds. By January 1985 the city treasurer, Mike Reddington, was forecasting that with contracts placed for building work worth £90 million, our capital budget – the budget which covered housing – would be £30 million in the red.

Jenkin and Baker must have thought they had us on the run. In fact Jenkin was so confident that he announced that unless we came up with a way of balancing the books he would block our spending on those contracts. Good old Patrick. What he could not have known was that for several weeks Tony Byrne, as chairman of finance, had been negotiating to find the money we needed.

On February 22nd, 1985 he played his trump card. He had found the £30 million – we were going to get it from a French bank, the Banque Paribas, in return for a deal by which they would take the money coming in from people paying mortgages to the council for houses which had been sold off over the years. It was brilliant, and floored Jenkin.

He had turned to the French for the deal because bankers in the City of London had become jittery, though God knows why. There's no safer investment than a city council, with all its assets in land and buildings, even if it is facing a financial crisis.

But not everything was plain sailing. Because we didn't want to break ranks with the London boroughs, Sheffield and the rest, we were still committed to setting no rate when Budget Day came along. To get maximum impact we had also agreed to bring our budget meeting forward to March 7th, 1985 to coincide with the others.

But just as we had forecast, when the time came to make their budgets, the others, with the exception of Lambeth, fell by the wayside. There was no concerted campaign.

Budget Day was almost a formality. Tony Byrne announced that we required £265 million for the coming year. But the Government said we must not spend more than £222 million. So, he announced, we would not set a rate – and we didn't. We knew there was no legal requirement to do so until June, so we postponed the decision until then.

But a move in the game which was totally outside our control was about to change events. The Audit Commission, whose job was to monitor local government finances, appointed a new district auditor, Tim McMahon. He took over from Les

94

Stanford. Stanford had warned the previous year about the dangers of surcharge and disqualification if we broke the law. But he had only warned us.

Now McMahon came down on us like a ton of bricks, and it was his report which would eventually land us in court, fighting the legal battle against surcharge and disqualification.

His appointment on May 1st, 1985 was the first step along that road, and on May 21st he wrote to us, warning that if we did not set a lawful rate, one in other words which would cover spending, by the end of the month, he would take action. He sent every councillor a copy of his report. It was only finding ourselves wrong-footed by the "no-rate" tactic which had left us out on a limb. But now we had been deserted by the other councils there was no reason for us to go on defending a strategy in which we didn't believe anyway, so we could go ahead and set a rate.

But there was no way in McMahon's terms that it would be lawful. To do that there would have to be a massive rates rise, and that was totally contrary to our policy. And there was no way that we would do it by his deadline of June 1st. Having been told on previous occasions that June 20th was the absolute deadline annually for rate-setting, we had already set June 14th, 1985 as Budget Day.

One option was to go for a twenty per cent rise, but Tony Byrne pointed out that even that wouldn't balance the books, and in any case the unions and the District Labour Party were absolutely opposed to an increase of that magnitude. So at a series of meetings in the run-up to Budget Day we hit on a figure of nine per cent for the rate rise.

But four days before the budget meeting, the bombshell dropped. Rate or not on June 14th McMahon was going for us anyway. He claimed that by not setting a rate by June 1st we had already incurred losses of the interest on rates which would have been levied. He calculated they amounted to £106,103, and notified us that he was going ahead with his move to hold us all responsible for that amount because of our "wilful misconduct". What's more, as the amount we were supposed to have lost the city totalled more than £2,000 for each of us, that meant we were liable for disqualification from office as councillors for a period of five years.

If we were all supposed to have been terrified by his threats, they in fact only served to harden our resolve to go ahead with the nine per cent rate rise, which would be interpreted as being unlawful. According to McMahon's assessment of the situation we had already broken the law. So what the hell had we to lose by doing it again?

This was to be the historic "illegal" budget. The Liberals screamed at us. The Tories ranted and raved. They insisted that we would not be able to balance the books, but we were adamant. We were sticking to our guns: minimal rate increases, better public services and more housing were what we had promised, and we intended to deliver. It was our problem, we said, to find the funds to make the books balance as the year went by. To a man forty-nine Labour councillors put their hands in the air, and the budget went through.

Twelve days later on June 26th, 1985 the district auditor served notices on the whole of the Labour group, apart from the "Scabby Six", telling us that action would now be taken against us to recover the interest on money lost to the city because of the delay in setting the rate.

We had stuck together, and all of us were convinced that there was nothing illegal in delaying the rate until June 14th. So the notices of surcharge were still a shock, of that there's no doubt, though I am not sure that we saw it as a serious threat. Certainly the idea that they really might disqualify us from office never entered our heads.

Once we had set the rate there was an obvious discrepancy between planned income and planned expenditure. We then had a responsibility either to accept the consequences of the shortfall, or to bridge the gap, which in real terms meant making cuts. Or we could take a stand, and reinvigorate the campaign to get more money from the Government.

The options were not exclusive, so Tony Byrne began a long running series of Finance and Strategy meetings to try and reconcile the figures. The press bayed at the door and hounded us. The opposition accused us of crisis management and lurching even further towards the very brink of city bankruptcy.

What they failed to understand was that the nine per cent rate was never intended to be more than a tactic. We knew that never in a million years would it produce enough money to carry through our plans, but it bought us time. It meant we had set a rate, albeit a notional one, and as far as we were concerned that meant we had complied with the law. The opposition argued that we hadn't set a rate in time, so we had broken the law.

The difficulties were immense. On the one hand the Public Works Loan Board – a body which advances cash to local authorities – could not hand over money until we presented certified accounts to indicate that our books were in order. So we could not borrow from them.

On the other hand the financial institutions in this country started rocking the boat as well. The problem was that no council can place orders for work to be done unless it can prove that it will be able to pay for it.

The situation was compounded by the Government policy of penalising high-spending councils. As long as we stuck to our guns on our budget policy, they penalised us and withheld grants. They refused to give us back the missing £30 million, and though throughout July and August Tony Byrne tried behind the scenes to negotiate with Whitehall to allow us to borrow money from the Public Works Loan Board, the Government dug its heels in.

So it was calculated that by December, unless a solution was found, we would run out of money.

That was when we took the fateful decision to issue redundancy notices to the whole of the council work-force.

EIGHT

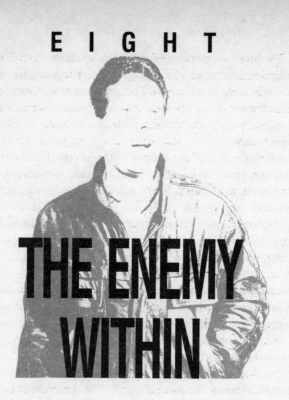

THE ENEMY WITHIN

The story of how a fleet of taxis delivered the redundancy no-tices to the council workforce in Liverpool is now legend. For the right-wing press it was a godsend. They were like hyenas gathered round a carcass. "So much for the Labour council which is committed to defending jobs and services," they crowed. "Look at them now – sacking council workers."

The redundancy notices were, of course, only ever in-tended as a technical device to give us breathing space in that September, 1985. The ninety-day notices would take us on to the end of December, and would keep us within the law. Our own officials pointed out that if we continued to employ people when the balance sheet said we would not have the cash to pay them, we would be breaking the law. But under the Employment Protection Act if we gave three months' notice we stayed within the law. Not that we ever intended sacking anyone, and let's remember that we didn't.

On September 6th, 1985 we announced the decision. How it backfired on us. The trade unions revolted, their national officials went for us, and at Labour Party headquarters the decision was seized upon as a stick with which to beat Militant.

We argued, that by issuing redundancy notices we could also hammer home the sharp reality of our arguments: that unless more money was available to Liverpool from the central funds, then jobs really were on the line. There was never ever any intention to implement a single one of those 31,000 redundancy notices.

So we went ahead and drew them up, and unleashed an animal reaction that we simply could not control. We had badly miscalculated. None of us ever thought the reaction would be so vicious, but the truth was that the trade unions no longer had the will to battle on with us in a new campaign for more money from Whitehall. Even their national leaders were publicly urging us to find a compromise solution.

We were paying the price for the months of inactivity when we went along with the London line of refusing to set a rate. From January through to June the workforce had watched us do nothing. The campaigning spirit had gone out of the fight. When suddenly we went for a nine per cent rate increase the shop stewards were four-square with us, but when we asked them to back us on the redundancy scheme the lid blew.

The next day, September 7th, the Joint Shop Stewards Committee met to discuss the plan. By a narrow majority they rejected the redundancy option. And I found myself in a head to head battle with a fellow Militant, Ian Lowes, a senior shop steward of the powerful General, Municipal, Boilerworkers and Allied Trades Union. Ian had been a key figure ever since we were elected in 1983. He worked as a tree-feller, but as chairman of the Joint Shop Stewards was in fact occupied full time on trade union activities within the council.

Now he went on record as saying: "We are not going to accept any redundancy notices. As soon as the first is issued there will be all out action." What's more I knew he had the power to stop us if he wanted. His members literally held the keys to the

Town Hall, the municipal buildings, and every other building in the city.

And on September 16th, 1985 they used them. We had called a meeting of the council to approve the redundancy notices. But when we arrived that morning the Town Hall was locked and barred – our own security force, Ian's members, had turned against us and were occupying the building. It was stalemate. We couldn't hold a council meeting, so we couldn't pass the resolution needed to issue the redundancy notices. The only thing left to do was try to persuade the trade unions to change their minds, and support us.

I will never forget the meeting of the Joint Shop Stewards Committee which followed. Tony Byrne and I tried to persuade them of the logic of the choice. To say it was a volatile meeting is an understatement. The white collar unions like NALGO, the Town Hall union, ranted and raved at us. Only some of the manual workers stuck with us.

We finally said to them, "All right, if you don't accept what we say, then what alternative tactics are there?" Unbelievably, from a meeting of Labour supporters who had gone down the line with us all the way, came the suggestion that we should capitalise: that we should take the money allocated, for instance, to the next year's housing programme, and use that to solve our problems. NALGO, under their senior shop steward Graham Burgess, pressed us to go for that option, even though we pointed out it would mean thousands of building workers going on the dole.

Eventually they adjourned their decision till the Monday, and the two of us went away unconvinced that they would hold the line.

When the meeting resumed they voted to back us, but the price we paid was enormous. NALGO, NUPE – the National Union of Public Employees – and the teachers' unions walked out and refused to vote. The Joint Shop Stewards Committee was split wide open, and the unions who were against us staged their own meetings and began the lobby against us.

100

The rest, the blue collar unions, accepted the redundancy tactic, and called for an all-out strike against the Government. In a ballot the move was narrowly defeated, and all that materialised was a one-day strike on September 25th.

The irony is that had those white collar union leaders who opposed us stayed and fought at that meeting, they could have carried the vote against us there and then, and the notices would never have gone out. Instead they chose to do a complete U-turn. Now we were their employers, and they fought us bitterly every inch of the way. We had told them that the redundancy notices were only a tactical ploy, but they sold the idea to their members as though it was for real. "Should we let our employers sack us – or should we stand and fight them now?" was the line they took.

I despise and hate them for what they did. At least their opposite numbers in NUPE were consistent. They had opposed our campaign from the start. NUPE has always been very much a right-wing manual workers' union, and they have never seen eye to eye with our policies.

Even against that background I was horrified by the turn of events. People who only ten weeks earlier had backed us every inch of the way were now attacking us. It was an about face which we had never foreseen. Even close friendships collapsed under the strain. I can think of one person, a very old and dear friend from my days at Goldsmiths' College in London, who in that year became anti-Militant, anti-Liverpool City Council, and took the side of the right wing of the Labour Party. His commitment, in truth, was not such that he needed to take sides. Mine was. So he chose to destroy our friendship and we have not spoken since. That is something I regret.

One thing didn't change. We still had to issue those notices, and we still had to find the money to bridge the gap. On September 27th, 1985 we sent letters to every one of our 31,000 workers breaking the news. There was the official notice from the city solicitor but we also sent a letter which John Hamilton and I signed in our capacity as leader and deputy leader.

In that letter we underlined the dilemma: "For our part we have always made it clear that unless the Tory Government provided resources commensurate with the cost of services then inevitably there would come a time when the money for wages and services would run out.

"The time has now come when this regrettable position has been reached. Obviously the steps we have had to take will cause concern and worry. However, this course of action provides the only way of providing wages and salaries until December 18th, 1985. Other steps would certainly result in the immediate cessation of payments and the cutting of services which we are pledged to defend. Furthermore this course of action gives the Government three months to negotiate with Labour representatives a just settlement to our financial crisis.

"If the Government recognises its responsbility then all notices will be withdrawn."

Some of the notices went in the post. Others were handed out in individual departments. But the ones which caused the greatest furore were those which went out by taxi. It was always standard policy to deliver notices of any kind to schools and colleges either in the council's own vehicles or by using a local taxi firm. So there was nothing underhand or unusual about it when we chose to use taxis to deliver batches of redundancy notices on this occasion.

But the press and the Labour leadership seized on it, and twisted it out of all recognition. It gave Neil Kinnock the chance four days later, on October 1st, 1985, to launch that vitriolic attack on me and Militant at that year's Labour Party conference in Bournemouth.

In my view it was a disgusting performance. He told the conference: "I'll tell you what happens with impossible promises. You start with implausible resolutions which are then pickled into a rigid dogma and you end up with the grotesque chaos of a Labour council hiring taxis to scuttle around a city handing out redundancy notices to its own workers."

He went on to blast Militant. He seemed to me to be clearly rattled and now any pretence there might have been of support for Liverpool was discarded. He told the conference: "I'm telling you, you cannot play politics with people's jobs, with their homes, with their essential services. They have no time for such posturing or for the generals of gesture, or for the Tendency tacticians."

Eric Heffer was so disgusted with Kinnock's attitude that he got up and walked off the platform. I stayed though I was bloody furious. Only a year earlier we had been the conquering heroes. Now Kinnock was denouncing us. But I knew even then – and how right I was to be proved – that the electors of Liverpool would make him eat his words.

Back in the city we still had to go on with the campaign against the Government for more money, even if we had been deserted by our own national leadership. We knew, though, that the writing was on the wall. We knew the campaign was coming to a close, and that the future was uncertain.

No one should underestimate the damage that was done by the split among the trade unions. They were without doubt the most powerful local authority shop stewards' movement in the land, and the one which had within it the greatest Militant influence. Because they were successful, they were also seen as a threat by their own full-time officials, men who saw their own power base being eroded.

They complained bitterly to me that they were no longer consulted, and that I was going behind their backs to deal directly with the shop stewards. They resented too the influence of Militant. Just as that influence had been growing within the Labour Party in the city, so it had grown within the trade unions, in no small way of course thanks to the efforts of Ian Lowes.

A lot of people have argued, though it is not the case, that Ian Lowes managed to prise more from a Labour council than he ever did from its political predecessors. They have said too that he used his position as a Militant to do that.

The truth is that there has never been an authority which took the workforce in as part and parcel of management in the way we did. They became part of the structure.

Conflict began when our approach to management differed from theirs, as it did in 1985. At that point you cannot expect local authority trade unions to be part and parcel of plans, for example, to use redundancy as a tactic.

In those kinds of situations the clashes I had with Ian Lowes were explosive. To be forced into making savings is, for a Labour councillor like myself, and a dedicated shop steward like Ian, who have both fought tooth and nail against making cuts of any kind, a very unpalatable situation. So at times Ian has been forced to behave like the hard-nosed convenor he is, rather than a comrade in the overall struggle.

Had it not been the case that we had spent so many years working for a common cause, and united under the flag of Militant, the conflict might have overwhelmed us. Even that mutual bond was sometimes placed under considerable strain.

Ian's single-mindedness could sometimes create more problems than it solved. He has always been unpredictable, and something of a rebel, and I would never know when he stormed into my office whether he was playing a political game, or playing the convenor defending the interest of his members against the council line.

I remember the blazing row we had when he ordered out the security force to seal off two depots in the city. They actually took over and brought work to a standstill.

Ian walked into my office, bold as brass, with all his troops in position, and told me what he had done. I was livid. We swore and screamed at each other and it very nearly ended in violence. It was only the years of working together, our common ground as Militant supporters, which prevented my office that day from becoming a real battleground.

In a way though that conflict is healthy. Even in a totally Socialist society there will always be the need for independent trade unionists. In the development of non-totalitarian systems you need trade union power, and conflicts are inevitable. But that is arguably better than the strain which unspoken anger can place on those relationships.

Whichever way we turned now we seemed to be running out of allies. The betrayal by the trade union leaders had brought me face to face with the stark reality of one political theory: the greatest obstacle to true Socialism is the leadership of the trade union movement.

Now, that October 1985, another so-called alliance crumbled. The Church turned against us, as Liverpool's two bishops wrote a letter to *The Times* condemning the tactics of Militant, and even suggesting that we should use money from the housing programme to solve the cash crisis.

The forces of Protestant and Catholic religions have long played a role in the politics of the city, and, as in Glasgow, even in its football. The sectarian divide has healed over the years, and when we came to power the Anglican Bishop of Liverpool, ex-cricket international David Sheppard, and the Roman Catholic Archbishop, Derek Warlock, offered a form of support.

The one thing which I think can be said of them both is that they lack sympathy for some of the Government's policies. David Sheppard, of course, came to Liverpool from the inner city areas of London, and perhaps his experiences there coloured his views of life and the role the Church should play. Derek Warlock too has always given the impression of feeling a keen concern for the plight of people in the most deprived areas of his city.

So when we came to power in 1983, campaigning for jobs and services, our "sermons" seemed to fall on receptive ears at both cathedrals. Long before they became involved with our campaign the two bishops had formed their own alliance. All credit to them in Church terms for the stand they took, because they were certainly subjected to criticism and opposition in many quarters from those who took the traditional view of the two religions.

In the first year, when we fired the opening shots in our campaign for more money for Liverpool, they showed some support. We met them frequently, and they used their connections to try and advance our claims. On one occasion

David Sheppard even went to dinner with Patrick Jenkin to spell out to him the plight of people in Liverpool.

It wasn't, incidentally, a tactic in which I had any faith. I always argued that you could sit and talk to Tory ministers all your life, but talking was no way to get money out of them. You get that when they see the thousands on the streets, and the action and strength which is behind those people. That is how you convince someone like Jenkin: not over the dinner table.

It was, however, a contribution which the bishops felt they could make. On one occasion the archbishop was so concerned to keep in touch that he literally caught me with my pants down.

It was on the eve of our meeting with Patrick Jenkin, and I was due to travel down to London to meet him, amidst rumours that he was going to settle and give us more cash, as he did. It had been a long hot day, and I was relaxing at home in the garden, wearing nothing but swimming trunks. The children were out, and Shirley was upstairs when the doorbell went.

I went into the house, opened the door, and came face to face with Derek Warlock in his full regalia. I just burst out laughing and said, "I'll bet you don't often get this sort of welcome." He just laughed, came in, and said he had simply called round to wish us luck for the following day. That was the sort of relationship we had then.

When it came to the battle of 1984–85 it was a different matter altogether. When things got tough, and we headed for a showdown in that second year, the bishops chose their side. I have to say that like so many others, when the chips were down they did not support us. When it comes to an "us versus them" situation I can think of few occasions on which the established Church has taken the side of a Socialist council against the Government.

When views polarised, and there was no middle ground left on which to stand, we lost their support. I can't pretend to be surprised. I don't believe that the Church as a body can ever be part and parcel of the struggle for the betterment of working class people let alone any fundamental change in society.

It confirmed the views I had begun to form back in those days of the Sixties at the Church youth club when after initially believing the Church might have a role to play in changing people's lives, I eventually became convinced that it was irrelevant. The events in Liverpool, and the stance taken by the bishops, only served to confirm that beyond a shadow of a doubt.

Talk about attacking from all sides! Don't forget that in the background the district auditor's move to surcharge and disqualify us was now a reality.

And we had so-called allies who were really the enemy within. National trade union leaders were deeply unhappy about the way things were going in Liverpool. They saw their power being usurped by the local shop stewards with our backing, and I was often accused of going behind their backs to solve the problems locally with the unions, while ignoring the national leadership.

It must not be forgotten that the motives of the top trade unionists in opposing us were much the same as those of Kinnock and the rest on the NEC. If we had succeeded in our campaign, then other local authorities would have followed our lead. That meant that the shop stewards' movement nationally would have gained power at the expense of the leadership. For trade union leaders who, as bureaucrats are very much part of the Establishment – often better at negotiating redundancy terms than they are at campaigning – it was a concept they could not swallow.

Yet now they joined an initiative which was supposed to help find an answer to the Liverpool finance crisis. David Blunkett, the leader of Sheffield City Council, had held out an olive branch after Kinnock's fearsome attack on us at the Bournemouth conference. In return for a deal under which I agreed to withdraw a motion demanding industrial action in support of councillors like ourselves who faced surcharges, he got together with leading trade unionists to help produce what was called the Stonefrost Report.

They appointed Maurice Stonefrost, a financial expert from the Greater London Council, who, along with three other local council money men, would go through our books and try to offer advice.

But Stonefrost came up with nothing new. His options all centred around a fifteen per cent rise in rates and involved cutbacks in the housing programme. Kinnock came out and said we should accept it. So did the trade union leaders who were part and parcel of this initiative.

There were the likes of John Edmonds, now the general secretary but then the assistant general secretary of the General and Municipal, who sat through all those meetings making encouraging noises, and was very much part and parcel of the democratic process. Then he switched his colours, and wrote editorials demanding our expulsion.

The same can be said of Alistair McRea, of NUPE, who also joined the witch-hunt. It was almost as though they were embarrassed that we had kept our word, and they had not. They didn't want us around to embarrass them further, particularly if a Labour Government came to power.

For my part I saw their actions as a betrayal. A betrayal not only of the Labour group, but of all those rank and file trade unionists who put their faith and confidence behind our campaign. We succeeded in so many ways: we created 6000 new jobs, we built 5000 new houses, we changed the education system, and raised the whole level of political awareness within the city. But we could have done so much more with the backing of the national leaders.

I often think that along with the Labour Party nationally they formed a barrier between us and the Tories. Mrs Thatcher did not have to move a finger to attack us. The job was done for her by the Labour Party leadership and the trade unions nationally.

On October 21st, 1985, only three weeks after Kinnock had reviled us at the party conference, he finally made the visit to Liverpool that we had urged. We were ready for him. We met for an hour and a half, but we made sure that we secretly taped what went on. It was the right move, because when after the meeting we announced that Kinnock now recognised our problems and was giving us his backing, he immediately denied it.

He held a press conference at which once again he lashed out at us. I sent him an open letter saying we must have been at two different meetings. It read: "For our part we all felt that our discussion was constructive and sympathetic. It seemed to us that you had recognised Liverpool's problems, that you were prepared to give support to the city council, that Kenneth Baker should visit the city and talk with its elected representatives.

"We of course recognised that there was a difference of opinion and that you suggested that we look at solutions within and without."

Then I went on to tell him: "Yet at your own press conference you seemed more intent on launching into a vitriolic and venomous attack on the city council. Our impression is that your concern is more with spearheading a witch-hunt than in attempting to solve the problems of Liverpool and its people."

A fortnight later Kinnock was to make a speech to the Fabian Society in which he paved the way for expelling Militant supporters from the party. While he was doing that our old enemies from the white collar unions in Liverpool – this time the National Union of Teachers and the National Association of Head Teachers – were fighting us in the courts over the redundancy notices, and the nine per cent so-called "illegal" rate. They won – the courts declared that both actions were unlawful.

The storm clouds were really gathering now. The consequences were that money to pay the workforce and the council's bills would run out in days.

On November 21st, 1985 Kinnock was at it again. We had warned that unless more money was available the city would have to run on emergency services only, and the council workers would have to go without wages. Kinnock threw the book at us, and made it clear he intended to "deal" with Militant.

We had our backs to the wall, and were heading for a tactical withdrawal. We had to balance the books to stay in office. I well remember calling Tony Mulhearn and Finance chairman Tony Byrne into my office and saying to them, "We are going to have to do something." Much as we hated it we were all realistic. We would have to take the step we had resisted all along, and go for capitalisation. Tony Byrne put the package together. We would take just over £23 million out of the capital account, but to ensure that housing programmes would not be affected we would also borrow abroad again – this time £30 million from Swiss banks. Other sympathetic Labour authorities had promised us the benefit of £3 million in loans they hadn't used themselves. And Tony managed to make savings of £3 million on our own spending. Put together the deal would pay the wages and keep the city running till the end of the financial year.

The plan went before the District Labour Party for approval, and on November 26th, 1985 went through the Finance Committee. The following Friday it was approved at the full council meeting.

The move was hailed as a climb-down by our opponents. They crowed that we had finally given in to the pressure to set a legal budget. Even I admitted it was a temporary setback, but without the backing of the national leadership, and deserted by the national trade union leadership, we had been left with no option.

But Kinnock wasn't through with us yet. On November 28th, 1985 the Labour Party's National Executive Committee announced that the Liverpool District Labour Party was being suspended pending an investigation, and there was to be an investigation into Militant.

Neil Kinnock said anyone proved to be a member of Militant would be expelled and made his now infamous statement: "It is generally recognised that Militant Tendency is a maggot in the body of the Labour Party."

NINE

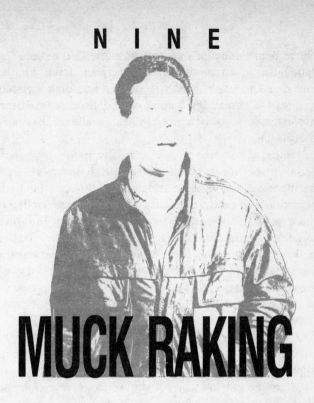

MUCK RAKING

If you believe what was written by the media about me during those three years in office, I was some kind of Mafia figure: a corrupt city boss, hanging on to power by bully-boy tactics, with a private army of thugs protecting me. The press never got tired of sniping at my "snappy" suits, the fact that I loved football, night-clubs, and enjoyed the company of women. They didn't like my temper and my arrogance let alone my political beliefs. The truth was, and still is, that I was an easy target, and they loved it. They saw me as Jack the Lad from Liverpool, with a ready answer for anyone and anything, and I didn't conform to their notions of Socialism.

But with rare exceptions, the press, and my political critics, never thought to ask themselves what made me what I am, and what makes me behave the way I do.

Yet Liverpool has always produced people like me, whether

it be in politics, football, comedy or music. Some people have argued that given conditions in Liverpool, those who have been born there fight harder to succeed and drag themselves up from the gutter. But similar conditions exist in Glasgow, in Newcastle and elsewhere, so that would be too simple an explanation.

I think it's more a case that Liverpudlians have an innate sense of pride about Merseyside. It breeds in them a determination that if they are going to do something, then they will do it better than anyone else. It's that philosophy which produced the Beatles, the Cilla Blacks, the Jimmy Tarbucks of this world. It also produces the Derek Hattons, the Peter Taaffes, the Tony Mulhearns. It's a natural spirit of competition, coupled with a belief that you're not simply as good as anyone else. You are better. It's that Liverpudlian arrogance which people found difficult to accept, but without it you can't win.

As for my violent outbursts, and the temper about which everyone talks so much, there is a degree of truth in it. I suppose I have never suffered fools gladly, and I came from a background as a kid where if you weren't prepared to tough it out, you were walked on.

I do remember, to my eternal shame, one episode when I was in London studying at Goldsmiths' College. I played football regularly for a team called Hornchurch up in Essex. One game in particular was a needle match. Win the game, and we would win the League. If we only managed a draw, then we were runners-up: and I have never given a toss for coming second at anything. Midway through the second half we claimed a penalty for a foul on our centre forward. As far as I was concerned the referee should have given it without hesitation, but he refused. I was furious, and without even thinking raced over and thumped him in the face. Looking back it was disgraceful, and these days I would criticise anyone for doing it. It was sheer frustration, and afterwards I apologised, but it was too late.

112

I was banned for life from playing in the Essex League – and rightly so.

It illustrates one of my failings. I do have a very short fuse, and if someone really gets in my way without good reason I'm likely to react violently without even thinking.

These days I try and keep it under control. There's nothing the press has enjoyed more than watching Derek Hatton lose his temper and lash out. Not that they have ever seen it happen during my television and radio appearances, because that is a much more controlled political atmosphere. If I do explode it is almost always over a personal matter, and often I lose my temper with the people I like and respect most. I was merciless with people who worked in the city council offices with me, but they knew that it was just the way I am.

I would very often shout and scream, then afterwards go along and give them a nudge or a hug, to acknowledge that I should not have behaved as I had. I don't find it too difficult to go back to someone with whom I've had the most incredible row, and say: "Come on, let's forget it." After all, I came from a family where on the surface there was a lot of shouting and aggression, but underneath it all we loved each other.

As for my ranting and raving against the opposition in the council chamber, that was different again. That was a political performance, staged for the benefit of other people who wished they were in a position to tell the Liberals and the Tories what they really thought of them.

There is no doubt that because I behave the way I do, and because of the success I achieved, I made enemies. There were threats against me, few face to face, and many anonymous. Yet when I hurled threats back those same people would go running to the press and accuse me of "bully-boy" tactics. Others tried to smear me, and of course, there were those who went further, and tried to have me convicted of corruption, with allegations that I had fiddled my expenses and that I had been involved in shady deals over planning applications.

That was one of the most distressing periods I have ever experienced. I can cope with being thrown out of the Labour Party, with losing the deputy leadership and with being thrown out of office. That is all part of the political battle. But the pressures that I faced during an eighteen-month-long police investigation into my personal finances had such an impact on me, and on my family, that I wouldn't want anyone else to have to face it.

For a year and a half from February 1985 onwards a chief superintendent, a sergeant and two constables from the Fraud Squad spent most of their time digging into my affairs in a way which few politicians can have experienced. They travelled across the world to places where I had been on holiday. They travelled the length and breadth of this country. They examined every scrap of paper, and every expense sheet I had ever submitted. No matter how innocent you are, the odds will be that as a human being, in filling out forms across a period of a year, there will be figures here and there which are wrong. That's not criminal: it's human error. But this was no ordinary investigation.

David Alton, the Liberal MP for Liverpool Edge Hill stood up in the House of Commons on February 5th, 1985, using his Parliamentary privilege, and tabled a motion urging the police to take action to investigate my alleged part in a planning application for a new hypermarket in the city. It all blew up because a Knowsley councillor, Tony Beyga, who is a long-time friend, was involved with the company making the planning application. What's more it was all absolute nonsense. I didn't have the power to put through a planning application by myself, and even if I had, I would not have been so stupid.

The newspapers loved it, and went to town with the headlines that I was being investigated by the Fraud Squad. Every time they ran a story about me in the months that followed they reminded their readers time and again that the investigation was still going on. Yet when I was cleared, and the Director of Public Prosecutions threw the whole thing

114

out, there were only paragraphs here and there. The press is clearly not impartial.

The first I knew of it was when a chief superintendent from the Fraud Squad rang and told me he had begun enquiries. Within a few weeks, he said, they would be calling me in to round it off. A few weeks! It was eighteen months before they spoke to me again, but during that time they talked to anyone and everyone they thought could help: my friends, my colleagues, people I had visited, and dragged them into the investigation. Not that I blame the police. They were simply doing their job. In my view, it was a vendetta inspired by political enemies who would have done anything to discredit me.

It was appalling. People I hadn't seen for years would suddenly ring me at home and say, "We've had the police round asking questions about you? What's going on?"

They went to see a friend in Birmingham to quiz him about a boxing evening I had attended. They dragged in the council press officer, Sue Hesk, and kept her for most of the day at the police station answering questions. They even tried to quiz the council drivers who chauffeured me around, to try and prove that I'd been abusing my position, claiming expenses which I hadn't incurred and using council vehicles for my own benefit.

Eventually, of course, they wanted to see me. I remember turning up on January 29th, 1986 at the Merseyside police headquarters which stands on the river front near the Albert Dock. I went with my solicitors, John Lindon and Keva Coombes. Both are old personal and political friends. John is a former Liverpool councillor. Keva was the chairman of the Labour-controlled Merseyside County Council before abolition, and was the Labour candidate for Hyndburn, in Lancashire, at the 1987 General Election. He was later to become the new leader of Liverpool City Council.

Talk about a stage-managed event! Within an hour of arriving the press and the TV cameras were camped outside. They were in for a long wait. Chief Superintendent Allen

115

Walker, head of Liverpool's Fraud Squad, was there, along with a sergeant and two constables. They started the tape recorders, and then grilled me until ten o'clock at night. They had collated expense sheets going back across two years, and would suddenly select one and ask me to explain it.

Then they expressed surprise that I couldn't remember all the details. Living the kind of life I do, I sometimes have problems remembering what happened yesterday, let alone two years ago. Who had gone with me to a particular meeting? Where did I stay? What meeting did I address? Bear in mind that during that period I would address four or five meetings a week, travelling all over the country.

They asked for my diary. I told them the only one I kept was a pocket diary which was in the office, and asked why they wanted it. "We can't make you hand it in," they said. "But if we arrest you we can demand it then." I went back to the office, got the diary and gave it them. I've never seen it since.

There were another two days of questioning like that. When they had finished the files went off to the Director of Public Prosecutions. I don't criticise the way the police did their job. They were hard, they were diligent, they were thorough, but they were fair. What I do criticise is a system which allows a man and his family to go through an investigation for so many months and have so little recourse at the end of it.

By the time they finished they must have had volumes of information about me, and what makes me so angry is that I've never been entitled to see it, nor have I been told what has happened to it.

The media had a field day, but that was nothing new, and when they ran out of steam on the fraud investigation, they could always fall back on one of their favourite topics – Hatton's Army.

The city council's static security force are the men responsible for security in every building the council owns, be it a building depot or the municipal offices.

Of all the things we did it was the one area which gave

rise to more myths and legends than anything else. Yes, they wore uniforms, which were heavy-duty green weatherproof jackets. Yes, they were loyal to us, and yes, some of them were heavy-looking lads, the sort who might handle themselves well in a spot of trouble. After all they were security men, not nursemaids. Some of them were, and are, Militant supporters but there are two thousand of those now in Liverpool. To hear the stories which were told you would have thought they were the praetorian guard, lined up and waiting to raise their spears against anyone who tried to challenge us.

There were occasions, I will concede, when some of them got out of hand, and went over the top, notably at news conferences, when the more militant among them, (and that's with a small "m") showed their resentment at the way the papers treated Liverpool. The press, of course, responded with their tales of "Hatton's Army" and the way in which it intimidated and harassed them. They ignored the fact that the papers for which they worked were in the main themselves hostile to Liverpool and the policies which had created jobs for many of those lads. Anyway the catcalls and abuse they sometimes got from the security force were no different from the normal rough and tumble of politics in Liverpool. It's no place for the faint-hearted.

The security force became what it was for two reasons. Before we took power there had been two sections, the static and the mobile forces. The men who controlled them were by tradition ex-police officers. Inevitably, because of their backgrounds, they tended to look on the mobile force as their blue-eyed boys, while the static force they regarded as simply night-watchmen. What's more, there had been a move under the Liberals, just prior to our take-over, to reduce the number of watchmen, and bring in private security companies to do the job.

The watchmen were members of Branch Five of the General, Municipal and Boilerworkers Union, under Ian Lowes, who as I have already described was a leading Militant in trade union circles on Merseyside.

As soon as we came to power in 1983 he put us under immense pressure to improve the lot of the static security force, to get rid of the private security elements which already existed, and to attach greater importance to the role of the static force.

He made immense sense when he argued that council buildings could be political targets for demonstrations and occupations by the political opposition. By strengthening the static security force, and giving them a higher profile, we could guard against political sabotage.

It was at that time that the first accusation of "jobs for the boys" came up. Eric Wright, the ex-bobby who had run the security force, was retiring, and we advertised the post. A whole number of ex-policemen applied, but we weren't happy. After all these men had good pensions, and didn't need jobs. Out there in Liverpool were people who were unemployed and who could do the job just as well.

Among the applicants was Dave Ware. Many of us knew him, myself included as he lived out in my part of Liverpool, three hundred yards away from my own home. We wanted someone who was tough and no-nonsense, and Dave seemed ideal. He was forty-four years old, married with seven children, and like many of the men who would be working under him knew what it was to be out of work. He had been unemployed for five years. He was a lad from the sort of Liverpool working-class background with which his own security force could identify. At the same time he could adapt to deal with anyone.

As soon as we announced the appointment at the end of September 1983 the balloon went up in the press. "Top job for Hatton's neighbour", they screamed. "Jobs for the boys". "Ex-bouncer gets security job". When he took over we spelt out our policy of beefing up the static force, and giving them a greater involvement. That only spelt more trouble, because many of the men in the mobile force were ex-policemen and resented what was happening. So the whole legend of the mobiles versus "Hatton's Army" was born.

It wasn't surprising, I suppose, that the men in the static force saw themselves as the elite. We had doubled their numbers, ended privatisation and given them an important role to play. We had created new jobs for many of them, so we now had a mass of people who felt a compelling loyalty towards us. They were clearly far closer to us than the rest, some of it personal loyalty, some of it political. But to suggest they were a private army who went into action every day, or acted as my personal bodyguard, is nonsense. Certainly they acted as my minders on some occasions. There were times when I needed that, especially during a period when there were threats towards me, and a whole series of vicious telephone calls to the house.

Some evenings, as a matter of course, members of the security force would call on Shirley and myself at home to check that everything was all right. Equally Dave Ware would come round sometimes to spend the evening with Shirley and me. He was never there as a minder, but it was comforting to know that if trouble did materialise he was close at hand.

A year later, on October 9th, 1984, it was "jobs for the boys" all over again as far as the press was concerned. This time the opposition were screaming and shouting about the appointment of a black Londoner, Sampson Bond, as principal race relations adviser.

Given that many people were, at that time, criticising our race relations policy, it was hypocritical that they should criticise the man we appointed to supervise its implementation. They didn't agree with the policy. They were, then, hardly likely to agree with our choice of the person best suited for the job.

Sam Bond was a twenty-six-year-old council worker from Brent. His own union, NALGO, and members of the anti-Militant black caucus of the Liverpool Race Relations Liaison Committee all criticised him for his lack of qualifications. Yet in race relations there are no such things as formal qualifications.

As Sam himself said in his own defence he had for years

steered clear of the "official" wing of the race relations industry. But in his job as a building surveyor with Brent Council he had gained grass-roots experience in fighting racism. He had an insight into the difficulties which could arise between a council, its staff and the trade unions in implementing a policy of equal opportunities.

He had fundamental differences, as he once said himself, with the so-called experts and professionals who worked in race relations.

It was the one issue which separated us from certain black groups in Toxteth. The day after his appointment a group of them even stormed into my office at the municipal buildings and virtually held me hostage for five hours, refusing to leave until we suspended his appointment. To keep them quiet and get them out of the building we told them we would readvertise the job. It was the only way of defusing the situation.

But next day, October 11th, 1984, the District Labour Party made it clear we had been forced to do that under duress, and the appointment stood. That became a bandwagon onto which the Church jumped as well. On November 14th, 1984, little over a month after Sam Bond was appointed, Liverpool's two bishops were still demanding that we freeze his appointment and reconsider it.

There were allegations that as a council we were racist, and were not doing enough in terms of either employment or facilities for the black population of the city.

The truth was, that we had a definite position on a very basic issue, that of positive discrimination. Certain individuals in the black community, in common with radical Church leaders and the trendy Left, like to argue that the black question has to be considered in isolation. The view of Militant, and that of the Liverpool District Labour Party, has always been that while accepting there is discrimination, the problems of the black community are part of the overall struggle. It is a class problem, and a Socialist problem, and must be solved within that wide framework.

To do otherwise is to alienate many white working-class people from identifying with the struggle. Had we adopted the policies of positive discrimination there would, I believe, have been a massive counter-reaction. How do you tell white kids out of work in inner city areas that the reason someone else has been given a job with the council is because they are black and you are white. That kind of quota system is intolerable. Black and white youngsters may have agreed or disagreed with the system we operated, but I never once heard them accuse us of racism. Had we gone along the road of positive discrimination undoubtedly charges of racism would still have been levelled against us, and I would have been hard put to deny them.

I make no apologies for the line we took. I still maintain to this day that it was the right approach.

So Sam Bond's appointment was vital to us. He took the Militant view of race relations, and it was the same view which had been thrashed out over the years in the District Labour Party. We had won the arguments there and we had won them at the municipal policy conferences. There was no way we were going to sacrifice them at that stage by appointing someone who did not share our views wholeheartedly.

Sam Bond was the only candidate who accepted those views without question. We would not have appointed a director of education who believed in private schools, or a director of housing who did not believe in municipal housing. So, while some individuals, and the press, howled their anti-Militant slogans, few if any of them bothered to examine the arguments which centred around our opposition to positive discrimination.

What really disappointed me politically though was the support that their arguments attracted within the Town Hall, where members of NALGO in particular refused to work with Sam. He was attacked at public meetings, and his colleagues in the union refused to recognise his appointment. They refused to connect telephone calls to his office and made his job impossible.

It's true to say that right through to the end of 1985 Sam Bond was a target for trade unionists who continued to boycott him, and prevent him fulfilling his role. He wasn't always in agreement with us on details. He wanted many many more blacks on the council workforce, and was deeply concerned that more wasn't being done to change the situation. But like us he believed that having a quota system was no answer. If all the energy which went into opposing him had gone into helping him, perhaps more would have been done.

The press, of course, especially papers like the *Daily Mail*, went to town on stories like that. By now they were painting me as a gangland boss with his posse of heavies. I wonder how some of those reporters would have reacted had they been on the receiving end of the kind of personal abuse my family and I received.

Mind you, I say papers like the *Daily Mail*. The irony is that the papers run by a man who proclaims himself one of the bastions of the Labour Party have spent more time trying to dig the dirt on me than most of the others. But Neil Kinnock shouldn't be too complacent about the strength of support he enjoys from Robert Maxwell and the *Mirror* group. He may use the *Mirror* as his daily mouthpiece for now, but those same editorials will be quick enough to turn on him if he steps out of line.

I well remember coming across Robert Maxwell in a restaurant in Bournemouth in October 1985 at the time of the Labour Party conference. As ever I couldn't resist having a go. Tony Mulhearn and I were having dinner with two journalists when Maxwell swept in and took over a table nearby. I turned to Tony Mulhearn and said in a loud voice: "Christ, he's even uglier close up than he is at a distance."

For the rest of the evening you could feel the vibrations coming from Maxwell's table. Ironically while I was sitting in Bournemouth in that restaurant with Maxwell, one of his hacks from the *Sunday Mirror* was out trying to do the dirty on me, knocking on the door of my home in Liverpool and asking my wife: "Do you know that your husband has gone to Bournemouth with a blonde, and what have you got to say about it?"

That is typical of the vulture-like attitude adopted by many journalists. I don't accept their glib excuse that they are simply doing their job. Doubtless some of them would have said that if they had been turning the gas taps on at Belsen. There are no depths they won't plumb, and whether or not they are telling the truth seems immaterial to them. Society and democracy are seriously undermined by that kind of behaviour.

They have given me hell in my personal life, camped outside the house at all hours of the day and night. I don't think anyone realises what that means for the children, who have had to cope with a lot. They faced newspaper headlines, reporters and photographers constantly harassing them and of course all the things that kids at school have said to them.

Having said that they seem to have become immune to it. I remember Becky looking out of the window one morning and saying, "Oh God, there's another flipping reporter outside."

Mind you there was one day when my temper did snap. It was at the time that the budget crisis was reaching its climax in 1985. I was leaving the house at breakfast time, when a freelance photographer working for the *London Evening Standard*, who had been posted outside for hours, leapt out of his car and began firing off shots at me.

I saw red, jumped out of the car and pinned him against the door. If I could have ripped the film out of the camera I would have done. It transpired later that he had been asked quite simply to get a photograph of me leaving for the office on Budget Day, but after all the harassment I had gone through I assumed he was yet another gutter journalist poking and prying into my private life.

I did apologise when I found out, but it would be so much simpler if journalists observed some code of ethics instead of behaving like Italian *paparazzi*. I sometimes wonder how my family life has survived it all – but Shirley has no doubts.

'When you consider the traumatic pressures we have faced as a couple at the hands of the media, and the pressure which that has placed on us as a family, it says a lot about our relationship that I can truthfully say that we never have rows, certainly not dreadful, bitter ones.

When things were at their worst the press were digging up any dirt they thought they could find. A reporter would appear on the doorstep with a photograph showing Derek with another woman. Another would turn up and say: "I'm so sorry to be the one to tell you this, but my editor has asked me to come and talk to you about your husband being seen with another woman."

Those kinds of situations produced a feeling of complete exhaustion. Not because they prompted rows between Derek and me, but because inevitably the whole family was drawn into it, and you spent time trying to keep them together. I would pick up a paper, read the dirt they were printing, and say to myself: "What a load of rubbish." But then my mum would say: "Well, there's got to be something to it. . ." and other people would react in the same way. It meant you had to spend time talking to them, and convincing them, and by the end of it all I was often emotionally and physically spent.

I remember spending one weekend at my sister's home while Derek was away at a conference in London, and thinking to myself that it was like being an actress on a stage. Life goes on. You still have to be at the school gate at half-past three, unless you are the emotional type who cannot face it. That's not me. I'm a battler.

I knew everyone had read the national press, and would be looking to me for some reaction, but I still wanted to turn up and pass the time of day with the rest of the mothers outside school. As far as I was concerned people could think what they liked but I was still Shirley collecting my kids from school, and as normal as anyone else.

What really annoys me is the way in which the media have tried to involve my children in their sordid little games. It's not in my nature to hate people, but given the experiences to which I have been subjected it's perhaps not surprising that I have a very low opinion of journalists and photographers.

124

One morning in particular Laura was ill, and couldn't go to nursery school, but I still had to take the other three. Carrying Laura, wearing her pyjamas and slippers, and ushering the other three along with me, I was trying to open the car door when I spotted two photographers lying in wait for us. One was in the garden next door, and the other at the bus-stop.

As I bundled the kids into the car I was saying to them: "Now when I pull out of the driveway put your heads down." Suddenly I thought to myself: "Christ, these are my kids. I'm only going up the road to school. Why should they have to start their day like this? What have they done?"

I pulled out and drove up the road to school, and there, hiding among the people at the bus-stop, among people who were my friends, my neighbours, my children's friends, were yet more photographers waiting to pounce.

So it's little wonder that until now I've flatly refused to talk to anyone about my life, my children or my husband. The only reason I have finally done so is that I can at least in my own words say what really happened, and people can perhaps understand the depths to which some papers will stoop, and the effect that can have on someone's life.

The fact that I would never oblige the media by performing for them even had its funny moments. Derek and I had gone out to the Adelphi Hotel in Liverpool for the evening to attend a charity boxing dinner. Television cameras from World In Action, who were also trying to dish the dirt on Derek, were hovering, and picked up a shot of the two of us leaving together.

The day after the programme was shown we had a telephone call from a close friend in Scotland, who had watched it with a few of his own friends. One of them asked: "Who was the striking blonde in the black dress with Derek?"

That did me the power of good! It might seem silly, but when you've been knocked and portrayed as the little woman at home – "Poor Shirley with the four kids" – then there's a little something inside every woman which says: "My God, I'll show them."

125

Of course it hurt when journalists arrived on the doorstep telling me that Derek had been seen with this woman, or that woman. You would be very cold and without feelings if it didn't. I well remember two reporters from the Sun *arriving on the day that they had run a particularly nasty and scurrilous piece. They had dug and dug, and had not been able to find anything in Derek's past which they could leech onto, and by that stage were prepared to go for anything.*

They stood there and one said: "I'm sorry if we have upset you." "Do I look upset?" I asked him. "Well, no," he replied. "There's your answer then", I told him, and shut the door.

How you feel when you do shut the door, walk back into the kitchen and put the kettle on, is another matter. I would think to myself: "Oh Christ, I thought all this had finished and died a death." But then I've learned to cope with it. Your emotions are topsy turvy, but under pressure you can either work well or collapse. I reckon I cope well under pressure, so those kinds of situations don't upset me but they do annoy me.

The way that a story is written, and the angle at which a photograph is taken, can portray something which is very far from the truth. Because of the commitment to the children at home I was seldom able to go with Derek to meetings and conferences. But he's the kind of person who loves having someone with him, and in fact needs to have company. So on many occasions simply the fact that someone else has been there in my place has fuelled the speculation and gossip.

So Derek and I have learned to sit down and talk those situations through. We talk for hours and hours, and because we are so close we always end up laughing.

I do find myself asking though, whether that is the best that responsible journalists have to do with their time. My life is my life, and I don't see why I should share it with everybody who opens a Sunday paper. It is very frustrating. After all my children are getting older, and I have to consider what they are thinking as well. On occasions where the press have been having yet another go at us I have asked them what has been said at school. Fortunately they are very lucky – they have very sympathetic teachers and very good friends.

The problem sometimes lies with the parents. No child is going to bother to sit down and read a newspaper story saying that Derek Hatton has been seen with one person or another. But you can just hear their mothers saying: "God, poor Shirley, I'm so sorry for her." So I have sat down and explained to the children as much as I can, and they are bright enough to work it out for themselves. Needless to say, as a result, they hate journalists with a passion!

Having said that, as even Shirley will concede, there are some journalists I regard as friends, and for whom I do have the utmost respect. True, they are in the minority. Most of them I simply suffer, and there are others I cannot tolerate and to whom I won't talk.

I did learn though, that while you may hate and despise journalists, it served no purpose to take it out on them in personal way.

It doesn't mean I haven't shouted at them, and called them all the rats under the sun, but I have developed a strange kind of love–hate relationship which I think has stood me in good stead.

For example David Davies, now one of the BBC's political correspondents, was the first man to interview me live on television. He is probably the most honest political journalist I have encountered. He has never taken our side, and has grilled me as hard as anyone I know, but he has always been honest, and has approached the issues in Liverpool in as fair a way as anyone could.

That first interview in 1983 was the one which, I suppose, sparked off my love affair with the television cameras. From then on television excited me. I enjoyed the pressure and the feeling of the adrenalin pumping. I suppose that's the actor in me again.

It has also given me some of my funniest memories of those three years in the limelight, appearing on everything from Robin Day's *Question Time* to *Wogan*.

Question Time was a programme which I always enjoyed. It was a challenge, knowing that the other three members of the panel would be against me and that Robin Day would give me a run for my money as he did on the first occasion I met him. I had been quoted in the *Liverpool Echo* as saying that "Robin Day had better remember that it's he who asks the questions and me who answers them."

Over the pre-programme dinner – always strange affairs because you are expected to discuss anything but politics – it became clear that he had read the comment. In typical Day style he then used it in his introduction.

The idea of those dinners was for the guests to have a drink, unwind and relax ready for the show. That just wasn't my style. I far as I was concerned they were serving me up as dish of the day, and I needed to take them on. So it was mineral water for me every time.

Any ideas I had of getting a head start by discovering what the questions were in advance went out of the window that first time too. I had taken the council press officer, Sue Hesk, with me to pump the researchers beforehand. For all the success she had she might have been trying to penetrate GCHQ at Cheltenham. The questions really are a closely guarded secret.

I also remember that first programme because I won myself a £20 bet. The previous Saturday, after going to Goodison Park to watch Everton play, I was in a pub in Liverpool, with a number of the players, including Adrian Heath. We were discussing *Question Time* and I jokingly said that somehow I would find a way of telling Robin Day that Adrian Heath should play for England.

I had forgotten all about it until it came to the end of the programme, the point where they finish the show on a lighthearted note. "With the exception of your own family, with whom would you most like to spend the weekend?"

was the question. As luck would have it, Robin Day went to the other three panellists first, as I sat there racking my brains for inspiration.

Suddenly the conversation in the pub came back to me, and the answer hit me like a flash. "Bobby Robson, the manager of the England football team," I piped up, "to find out why he doesn't pick Adrian Heath for England."

Typical of me, I suppose, that even on Robin Day's programme I should manage to mix politics with the other love in my life – football.

T E N

TRUE BLUE HATTON

It's just as well that the labels I've had in the world of soccer have no relevance to my political activities – because football is the only place where I can be described as a true Blue: I'm a devoted and fanatical Everton supporter.

What's more when I play football you'll usually find me on the right wing! As schoolboy footballers go I was hardly a star, but I was rated as a useful player in those days at the Liverpool Institute, where I did so little academic work that they wanted to throw me out.

It was when I came back to Liverpool, from 1972 onwards, that I really started going to Goodison Park again on Saturday afternoons to watch Everton. That was a really lean period for them, and though you would never deny your colours, in an argument it wasn't something you went around shouting about.

From then on football was almost as much a passion in my life as politics. Mind you, on Merseyside they take their soccer very seriously. It was Bill Shankly, the dour little Scot who was a legend as the manager of Liverpool Football Club, who once said: "Football's not a religion in Liverpool – it's more important than that." He was right. I once said myself that I could cope with being thrown out of the Labour Party, with losing my job and with disqualification as a councillor but I couldn't handle Liverpool beating Everton four-nil, and Ian Rush scoring a hat-trick against them.

It's true that even at the times of greatest political crisis on the city council, I would never miss going to a match, whether it was on a Saturday afternoon, or a mid-week evening game. Not that I was any different from most other councillors in that respect, no matter what their political colours. If Liverpool or Everton had an evening fixture on the day that the city council was sitting you could be certain that the meeting would end by half-past six – it was amazing how much business you could get through to make sure you were there in time for the kick-off.

Football has always shone on Merseyside even when times are bad. People always look to it to fill the gap in their lives, and the way their team is performing can affect everything else they do. In the days when the docks were going strong it always used to be said that the work rate on a Monday was directly related to Everton or Liverpool's result the previous Saturday.

But no matter what the result, no true Merseyside football fan would ever dream of changing his loyalty to his team, even if they were going through a bad patch. That was certainly true for me in the late 1970s when Gordon Lee took over as manager at Everton.

In my view Lee didn't know how to utilise the talents at his disposal. He had players there like Duncan McKenzie, who must be one of the cleverest footballers I've ever seen on the field, yet Lee didn't use him in the way he should have done.

I remember playing a charity game with Duncan only a year or so ago, where he scored one of the most memorable goals I have ever seen. He ran down the midfield, paused in front of the goalie, spun on his heels, trapped the ball between his legs and flicked it back over his head and over the keeper. Then he ran round and popped the ball in the net.

Afterwards he came up to me, grinned, and said: "If Gordon Lee was managing me now he would have given me a roasting for not passing to someone else!"

In 1981 Howard Kendall was appointed manager, and from then on I began to strike up a personal relationship and friendship with the club and the players. Within about two months the club had been revitalised. Peter Reid joined the side, Adrian Heath was on song, Andy Gray was signed and Colin Harvey become first team coach.

Ask any Evertonian and they will tell you about the famous Adrian Heath goal at Oxford late in the 1983–84 season which gave us a replay in the League Cup. From then on the club never looked back. Peter Reid developed into the world class midfield player that he is, and Andy Gray became an inspiration to everyone in the side. Much of the credit has to rest with Kendall. He was a brilliant manager, and together he and the team were a formidable combination.

I love nothing more as a relaxation than going to Bellefield, the Everton training ground, talking to the lads and the staff there. For me it is a real retreat.

So that love of football, that passion for Everton, has always been there one way or the other, and has been passed on to my son Ben, who is a better player than I ever was, and never misses coming to the match with me. People often ask me what I would do if I wasn't in politics. I tell them, and with a degree of seriousness, that I would have loved to have been a football commentator.

While I find football fascinating there are parts of the game these days which I dislike. It has reached the stage where it is now such a big business that money dictates almost everything. Smaller clubs find themselves going to the wall, and the box-office mentality rules the day.

I think it is criminal for instance that the unemployed now find it quite a struggle to find the money to go to a match. Ticket prices in some cases have reached unacceptable levels.

Violence on the terraces, too, has badly damaged the reputation of football, and of course, we in Liverpool have our own particular cross to bear in that respect.

The deaths of those thirty-nine supporters at the Heysel Stadium in Brussels, during the European Cup Final between Liverpool and Juventus on Wednesday May 29th, 1985, is something all Merseyside football fans will remember with horror to the end of their days.

On the night it happened I was at home watching the game on television. I couldn't believe what I was seeing. It was like a nightmare as the fighting on the terraces broke out, and a wall collapsed. Fans were crushed to death as it fell, or were killed in the panic which followed. Within minutes the telephone went, and Press Association were asking for my comments. Within the hour it seemed that half the world's press and television stations were at the door or on the phone.

I realised as the reactions poured in over the next few days that as a city we ought really to mount some kind of public-relations exercise to demonstrate that we were as shocked and concerned as everyone else. I discussed it with fellow councillor Peter Lloyd and with the council's chief executive, Alfred Stocks, who began making telephone calls to Turin to try and set up some kind of visit. He also made contact with the Anglican and Catholic bishops of Liverpool.

Soon we had arranged for a delegation to travel out to Turin, where we met civic leaders and attended a memorial service. The visit undoubtedly served its purpose, and was genuinely appreciated by the Italian people as well as the Italian authorities. There were no words of reproach, simply a spirit of reaching out, especially when we met the relatives of some of those who died. It made you realise that the level of bitterness and anger portrayed by the media had to be questioned, and that in the minds of the ordinary people who had suffered, the question was one not of retribution, but of why it had happened in the first place.

Indeed the mayor of Turin, Giorgio Cardetti, told us: "This act of reconciliation on your part is an act of courage and humility that we especially welcome. Let us work together to ensure that there will be no more absurd tragedies like Brussels."

The reasons for the mission were twofold. There was naturally the feeling that because the name of Liverpool was being dragged through the mud we should react, as a city council, to that situation. Then there was my own love of soccer, matched in many cases by others on the council. Having said that, I believe the Belgian authorities had to shoulder their share of responsibility. Conditions inside that stadium would not have been tolerated at a third division ground in this country, yet the Belgians seemed quite determined to place all the blame at the door of so-called Liverpool supporters. The Football Association and the European Football Association too must accept that they were the ones who allowed the match to go ahead under conditions which were deplorable.

Make no mistake, though, I always believed that if anyone calling themselves a football supporter carried blame for what happened on that night they must be made to pay the penalty. I don't believe that a single Liverpool supporter went to Brussels with the intention of killing a single Italian supporter.

But you also have to ask, looking at the level of violence in soccer as a whole, what promotes it. I believe you must accept that conditions in society contribute to that kind of behaviour. The feeling of hopelessness which exists among unemployed youth today is bound to cause a backlash and find its outlet in other ways. Behaviour on the soccer terraces is a part of the evidence that this is so.

I do get angry when I hear sports commentators and government ministers pontificating about violence on the pitch, and arguing that this in some way has a knock-on effect on the terraces. There is ample research to show that this is not the case. It also ignores the fact that many players, among them the Everton squad, are now throwing their weight behind the campaign to stamp out soccer violence.

The irony is that in their own derby games, and in their trips to Wembley, Everton and Liverpool supporters are an example to the rest of the country. Someone asked me some time ago whether they would be safe taking their son to Goodison Park for the local derby match, as a birthday outing. I told them what I tell everyone: "You could safely let him go by himself."

I always remember the comment made by an assistant commissioner of police at Wembley before an Everton–Liverpool Cup Final. It was the only occasion, he said, on which he had been able to give his men leave, rather than having to draft in reinforcements. That, I feel, said everything, though I doubt whether it merited a mention in the press.

Like any true Blue I wouldn't dream of missing a Wembley final, no matter what was happening on the political front! I always take my son, my father and a couple of friends with me. The atmosphere, if you have never been, is indescribable, no matter what the result.

My position on the council meant that I was able to meet the players and management at Goodison Park on the kind of terms that would never have been possible years ago, and for that I'm enormously grateful. Many of the lads have become close friends, and I often see them for a drink or meet them while they are training. Obviously there are some for whom I have particular admiration, and Peter Reid is certainly one of those. I think he is probably one of the greatest midfield players ever to lace a pair of boots, and in the Mexico World Cup in 1986 he transformed the England squad.

Soccer apart, his whole attitude to the game is an inspiration to young players and young fans. Strangely though, in that great Merseyside tradition of divided soccer loyalties, his whole family with the exception of his mother were Liverpool supporters. Peter always says his mother was the only one with any common sense. The rest only changed sides when he signed for Everton. I had the same discussion with Peter's father who said that until Peter signed for the Blues he could never have imagined himself going to Goodison Park to watch a game, and how he had to choke down the inclination to shout for the Reds.

One of Peter's other great fans is Brian Clough, the Nottingham Forest manager. I'd always been intrigued by "Cloughie's" reputation, and on one occasion decided that I really ought to meet him. Everton were playing Forest, so I said to my secretary: "See if you can get Brian Clough on the phone for me." I think she thought I had gone mad, but I knew that he had a reputation for being politically sympathetic. During the miners' strike he actually gave out free tickets to the strikers, and, having heard that he was a member of the Labour Party, and very much a Socialist, I wanted to meet him.

In addition I have always viewed him as a great football manager, and a man who talks great sense about the game. He was delighted to go along with the idea, and on the day we met, he instantly confirmed my belief about his political sincerity, and his knowledge of soccer.

I think it's fair to say he is more on the right wing of the Labour Party than I am, and his big concern was that we should first see a Labour Government returned to power before we set out about making any changes within the party. That is of course a view I don't share. I believe that we should be sustaining the pressure for change now, and that the policies put forward by Neil Kinnock are not the ones which will attract the support of ordinary working-class voters.

We talked football too, of course, and I introduced Brian to Peter Reid's father who was with me. Both of us laughed when Cloughie, who is a great Peter Reid fan, confessed that he had told the Notts Forest team at half time: "Peter Reid is obviously carrying a bit of an injury – just imagine what he would do to us if he was fully fit!"

Andy Gray too was a player who has inspired everyone with whom came into contact. I admire the way he conducted himself both on and off the pitch, and his controlled aggression on the ball was a joy to watch. He gives everything he has for football, and a bit more besides.

Among other players whose names would have to feature on any Everton roll of honour are Kevin Ratcliffe, Graeme Sharp, Trevor Steven and Neville Southall. For my money too, until the incident on New Year's Day 1986 when a leg injury put him out of the game for two seasons, Paul Bracewell was the best midfield player in the country.

Couple that kind of genius with the managerial and tactical flair of Howard Kendall, the dedication of an ex-player like Colin Harvey as the trainer, and the skills of Terry Darracott who coached the reserves, and you had a great club. When Kendall left Colin Harvey stepped into his shoes to continue the world beating Everton tradition.

One of my fondest football memories is in fact tied to a defeat. It was the weekend we were beaten 3-1 by Liverpool at Wembley in the Cup Final in May 1986. As an Evertonian I had my head in my hands. Not only had my team lost, but it also gave Liverpool the double – both the League and Cup titles. As a civic leader I had to go ahead and organise a homecoming for both the winners and the losers. I flew back to Liverpool to be there in the welcoming party when the two teams arrived, and I should have been on board the civic bus in the centre of the cavalcade.

There was no way I could do it. I knew my place was on the Everton team coach, with the lads, who were still holding their heads up even though they had lost. It was a very emotional drive, but I like to think the team were glad to have me on board. Certainly one thing I do remember: winners or losers the entire population united behind Liverpool's achievement, and the great name the city has given to football.

It only served to confirm my belief that football is one of the finest sports on earth, and nothing would give me greater pleasure than to see my son go on to a professional career in the game, so long as it was with Everton!

ELEVEN

THE WITCH-HUNT

Of all the years I spent in politics in the city of Liverpool none was to have more far-reaching implications than 1986. I had started out in life on the wrong side of the tracks back home in Childwall and worked my way to the top of the political heap. Now forces were gathering to drag me down again.

At the turn of the year the Labour Party investigation into Liverpool was well under way. A nine-man inquiry team had arrived on Merseyside and the rats were coming out of the woodwork to give their so-called evidence – evidence which they hoped would have me thrown out of the party along with other Militant supporters.

Four months earlier, in September 1985, the district auditor had fulfilled his threat to surcharge and disqualify myself and the forty-six other Labour councillors for allegedly failing to set a rate in time, and losing the city £106,000. A High Court appeal against that decision was to take place in the New Year.

The police investigation into my council expenses was continuing, and my bosses in Knowsley were moving to have me sacked because they still resented the amount of time I spent away from my job on Liverpool City Council business. But I wasn't going down without a fight for my personal and political life. We were still waging war with the Government over Liverpool's finances, and the city council elections, at which we would put our beliefs to the test with the voters, were due again in May.

So a by-election in the Old Swan ward, as a result of the death of fellow Labour councillor Peter Lloyd in the Spanish car crash, was seen as a crucial test of our popularity. Voting was on Thursday, January 9th, 1986 – and we lost. I admit it was a blow. Peter had been returned with a 990 majority in 1984. Now the Alliance beat us into second place by almost the same majority. The Liberals had made Militant a bogeyman during the campaign, and used every dirty trick in the book. The media were biased too. But we had to concede that it was a setback.

More was to come. On January 14th, 1986 we travelled to London, to the High Court in the Strand, where three judges were due to hear our appeal against the £106,000 surcharge, and a five-year disqualification as councillors. The Lambeth Labour councillors – now the only other council left in the fight – were also due in court that day. We travelled down overnight in a hired coach, and then joined forces with them.

Together, before the hearing began, we marched through London to the Houses of Parliament, with banners flying to demonstrate our protests.When the court hearings began it was decided that Lambeth's case should be heard first. Ours would not start until the beginning of February.

Meantime back in Liverpool itself, the Labour Party inquiry team were still taking the evidence they would present to the National Executive Committee in support of the calls to have us expelled from the Party. I had already been called to give evidence myself in January, and on February 16th, 1986 at the final session, I went before them for a second time. It was outrageous. They were preparing nothing more or less than a show trial, and were prepared to listen to gossip and innuendo from any quarter in their desperation to deal with Militant. There were allegations of bully-boy tactics. There were claims that we had usurped the authority of the Labour group, and, of course, there was the old old cry that we were operating as a party within a party.

All this at a time when it was becoming clear that a General Election was looming. Neil Kinnock should have been concentrating his efforts on uniting the Labour Party. Instead he seemed intent on destroying it.

On February 24th, 1986 the witch-hunt intensified. The inquiry committee made their report public, and, what a surprise, they were recommending our expulsion. Kinnock, of course, denied it was a witch-hunt, but then he would. But he must have realised how high feelings were running when two days later he turned up at the Labour Party headquarters in Walworth Road, London, for the meeting which voted to press charges against myself and fifteen others from Liverpool. He had to have a police escort to get into the building. Hundreds of us stood outside barracking him as he arrived.

On March 5th, 1986 came the next blow. The High Court ruled that both we and the Lambeth councillors were guilty of wilful misconduct in not setting a rate in time. We were to be thrown out of office, and each and every one of us faced huge legal costs – and surcharge bills. Now we only had one chance to save our political skins. We would appeal to the House of Lords. But what price justice in Maggie Thatcher's Britain? The forty-eight of us already faced a bill of £350,000 for the High Court action. To go on to the House of Lords would cost another £250,000. Those sections of the Labour movement which supported us were doing all they could to help raise funds, but it was a drop in the ocean compared with the final price. Bankruptcy was staring us in the face. So too was expulsion from the Labour Party.

By March 11th, 1986 the NEC had dropped the accusations against four of the sixteen of us from Liverpool. So now twelve of us were left facing charges that we were members of Militant, had broken Labour Party rules, and had acted in such a way that we would bring the party into disrepute. The hearings at Labour Party headquarters were set to begin on March 26th, 1986. But it was to be another kangaroo court. We were even to be denied the right to have a solicitor present. It was, as I had always forecast, to be a show trial. They had already decided we were guilty.

So we decided to use the same weapon that had been used to try to get us thrown out of office. We went to the High Court. Our claim was simple. We were being denied natural justice. We were not to be allowed legal representation at the NEC hearings, nor were we to be allowed to cross-examine witnesses who had given "confidential" evidence to the inquiry team. On March 25th, 1986, just twenty-four hours before the NEC was due to sit, we were vindicated. The High Court judge who had heard our application for an injunction ruled that the way the NEC planned to stage the hearings was "manifestly dangerous". The confidential evidence – just another phrase for gossip, tittle-tattle and lies – could not be used.

More than that, members of the inquiry team would be barred from sitting on the disciplinary panel. It was that ruling which paved the way for one of Neil Kinnock's most embarrassing moments. Next day, March 26th, 1986 the NEC sat down to consider our case. There would have been twenty-nine of them at the meeting. But the eight members of the inquiry team after the court ruling were barred from taking part. That left twenty-one members of the National Executive at the meeting.

According to Labour Party rules it took fifteen people to make a quorum, so there was still no problem in going ahead.

But to Kinnock's fury, our old friends on the Left stood by us to a man. Eric Heffer and Tony Benn led a walkout by seven members of the NEC in protest at the witch-hunt. Which meant Kinnock was left with only fourteen people round the table. The hearing could not continue!

I will always remember standing on the steps outside the offices in Walworth Road, besieged by a massive crowd of triumphant supporters. Tony Mulhearn and I stood shoulder to shoulder, raising our fists in a victory salute as the crowd sang "The Red Flag". It was magnificent.

Kinnock was livid. His outbursts later to the media said it all. He described the walkout as sabotage and as a pathetic and infantile protest. But there was nothing he could do. The hearings had to be postponed. It was a brilliant victory.

But another even more important victory was just around the corner. We were now in the run-up to the city council elections, due to take place on May 8th, 1986. This was the real test. If the people of Liverpool voted to back us after all that had happened, Kinnock's nose would be well and truly bloodied.

Not that the Labour leader was through with us yet by any means. His first moves to expel us had been thwarted, so now he moved the goalposts. On April 19th, 1986 he persuaded the NEC to change their rules. Now they didn't need fifteen members of the NEC to constitute a quorum. In future it would only take half the number eligible to attend at any meeting plus one for that to be legitimate. Having done that, they went ahead and ordered the witch-hunt to resume in mid-May.

On May 23rd, 1986 another weight was lifted off my shoulders. I finally heard that the police investigation was over. Files had been sent to the Director of Public Prosecutions, and, as I had claimed all along, I was in the clear. All the allegations of fiddling my expenses and corruption had been tossed out of the window. My political opponents were furious. Another chance for them to smear me in the May election had just gone out of the window. Some of them still tried. There was an attempt to involve me in fresh allegations about planning applications. But it was all mud which would not stick.

The proof was there for everyone to see when the results came in on election night on May 8th. The Tories were wiped out by the Alliance. They lost six of the seven seats they were fighting. We lost two seats to them as well – but we also won two of theirs, and won a vacant seat as well.

So in spite of all the mud which had been thrown at both a personal and a political level, in spite of everything that had been done by Kinnock and the courts, the Liverpool Labour Party was still in complete control of the city, and now had one more member on the council than before. It was one of the greatest moments of my life to walk down into the basement of the council offices on the night of the count, and say to a crowd of journalists: "Does anyone want to count the votes again?"

The only sad note from my point of view was that during the weeks of the election campaign another friend who had stood with us against the Government had died. The death of sixty-seven-year-old councillor Bill Lafferty meant that there were now only forty-seven "rebel" Labour councillors left fighting the battle against disqualification.

There were also now only eleven Liverpool Labour Party members left fighting the battle against expulsion. The NEC had withdrawn their charges against thirty-one-year-old Richard Knight for lack of evidence. And with three others unable to attend, there were only eight of us left when the date set by Kinnock for the resumed NEC hearings, May 21st, 1986, came round.

The purge was about to begin. The first to go was Tony Mulhearn. On May 22nd, 1986, after twenty-three years' loyal service to the Labour Party, he was expelled. They still refused us the right to have a lawyer present or call witnesses. Tony did not even stay to hear them pass judgement. I didn't even stay that long. I stormed out at the very start and warned them that if they passed judgement in my absence I would go back to the courts to have their decision overturned. That stopped them in their tracks.

But the cat and mouse game of putting off the day of judgement could only go on for so long, and eventually they called my bluff, and went ahead without me. Kinnock was determined to have my head on a plate and the NEC disciplinary hearing at Walworth Road, on June 12th, 1986, was to be the moment he had sought for so long.

143

Tony Benn and Eric Heffer fought our corner again, demanding an adjournment. But Kinnock was determined to have his way. Unknown to most people a tape-recording was made of that hearing. Until now its contents have never been made public. But listening to the tape, it appears in my view that Neil Kinnock was prepared to go to almost any lengths to rid the Party of me.

It had been clear to me from the moment the national trade union leadership turned against us in the summer of 1985, that it was only a matter of time before the Party leadership, in the shape of the NEC, mobilised against Militant as well. Once they had decided they were going to do that, it was then again only a matter of time before they attacked us individually.

We were determined to make it as difficult as possible for them and used every trick in the book to try and delay the hearings. The more time we could buy for ourselves, the harder we made it for the NEC, and the more we could expose them as the political nondescripts I believe them to be. It had always been predicted that the NEC would take on the editorial board of Militant, and expel them as they did. In that way they had acknowledged that Militant should not stay within the Party, and created the psychological mood for the battle against us. I don't think we had ever believed they would pick off the rank and file. Now we had our backs to the wall, but we still had our supporters within the NEC.

Tony Benn has always been a loyal friend of the Left. The truth is that had he taken the support of Militant publicly a long time ago, then Kinnock might not be leader now. So it was no surprise to find Tony in there at the start, moving an adjournment on the grounds that I was an elected councillor, that I was the elected and recently re-elected deputy leader of Liverpool Labour group, and that I was only absent from the hearing because I was acting in the interests of the city – tied up in a series of important meetings – and following policies which had been implemented by the Labour Party conference.

What was more, he said, a hearing in my absence might seriously prejudice my chances of a fair hearing in the rate-setting row, which at that time was still due to come before the House of Lords.

Eric Heffer seconded the adjournment motion. It had come to something, he said, when as a member of the NEC he had to find out about the meeting by reading the *Liverpool Echo*. He had never been consulted about the date of the hearing, and he was deeply unhappy that myself and others, due to face disciplinary action, should be disadvantaged by hearings which coincided with two vital Finance Committee meetings in Liverpool.

The NEC already had before it a letter from my lawyers, asking for the adjournment. It was, said Heffer, a most reasonable letter. After all Liverpool City Council did have extremely difficult financial problems, and were again faced with the demands for cuts in spending. He pointed out that we were in almost permanent session, and our two days of financial meetings were crucial. He told the hearing they should accept there were circumstances beyond everyone's control. Of course I wanted to be there, said Eric. The letter from my solicitors made that plain. It said: "Derek Hatton does indeed wish to attend the NEC for the hearing so that he can answer the serious charges that have been brought against him. Our client believes the charges can be answered in full if he is given a fair hearing."

Of course, Larry Whitty, general secretary of the Party, was having none of it. He admitted the dates set for the NEC hearings had leaked before the official notices went out, and claimed that my response had been to say I would be on holiday. Not that Larry Whitty had ever asked me: simply that he was prepared to believe what he read in the papers.

He even implied that the Finance Committee meeting dates were just an excuse for me to stay away. "It seems to me unlikely that at the point where Mr Hatton clearly knew the date of this hearing he had a fixed date for these finance meetings in his diary. That's all I want to say," said Whitty.

That's all! There he was virtually calling me a liar, trying to blacken my case, and blatantly trying for a hearing without me, yet he sat there saying that justice was being done.

Alex Kitson, the deputy general secretary of the Labour Party at that time, was at least more up front. He told the hearing: "I know if I was being flung out of the Labour Party or being threatened with it I would make sure of my priorities, and mine would be here.

"I wasn't born yesterday and maybe a game is being played here. But even despite all that, we have a situation where if we go ahead with this case in his absence there will be prejudice and campaigning against us, regardless of what the result. People can point the finger at us and say Derek Hatton wasn't there. He asked for a reasonable adjournment and didn't get it. That's the game that's being played and that's the way it will come out. I would make a plea, despite all the prejudices we've got – and maybe doubts – that we should bend over and support the motion for an adjournment to a later date."

Just listening to the tapes now makes my blood boil. All we wanted was a fair trial and natural justice but Kinnock had made up his mind we were going, the Right were in control, and it's clear looking back that it didn't matter a damn what was said.

Dennis Skinner, the Labour MP for Bolsover, hit the nail on the head. He told them: "These are very important questions which affect some people's continued membership of the Labour Party. Like Eric Heffer I've had to pick up the paper to find out what's happening and when we're meeting. I believe that these meetings are being fixed in order to ensure that there's a right-wing majority when they are held.

"I believe that on the two previous occasions when ordinary National Executive meetings have been adjourned and then re-convened on a different day, it's been done in the main because some people on the right wing have said it's been convenient for them to attend on that day.

"So I believe Derek Hatton is perfectly right to say in line with others, I can't attend – I've got some other business, when he has complained about the date of the meeting. If I was a city councillor and deputy leader, facing such a crisis, I would have to seriously consider whether I could be at a meeting of this nature."

There's one thing about Dennis Skinner. He never minces his words. Like his brothers David and Graham, two of the eleven Clay Cross Urban District councillors from Derbyshire who were suspended from office in 1974 and later made bankrupt for taking illegal action against the Housing Finance Act, Dennis sticks to his principles.

He gave it them straight. "I believe these meetings are being fixed in order to ensure that there's a majority to expel.

"In Parliament MPs, Shadow Cabinet Ministers, Cabinet Ministers, when we're in government, find that they can arrange meetings to suit themselves.

"Some MPs are not only allowed to be absent for important debates but they are also allowed to take a Tory with them to ensure the balance.

"In other words it is a case of double standards. Across there at the Palace of Westminster, it's quite usual for meetings to be arranged in order to suit the individual concerned. So I believe that Derek Hatton has a perfect right as chairman of his personnel committee and deputy leader of the council, to make a request to have his case heard on a later date.

"I don't like to hear that a city in crisis can't have important meetings on two successive days. I talked to my brother, who tells me that during the Clay Cross crisis, when they were fighting the Heath Government and the Housing Commission, they once had four meetings in a week."

Neil Kinnock was having none of it. He dived straight in, saying that my solicitors had been given the notice of the NEC meeeting on May 29th – yet the notice of meetings with the trade unions in Liverpool and the meetings of the Finance and Strategy Committee hadn't been sent out till some days later. The implication was that we had rigged the dates of other meetings to block the NEC hearing. Of course we hadn't, but neither had we tried to change them to accommodate the NEC.

Typically he tried to rubbish the question of whether fellow Militant Felicity Dowling and I needed to be at crisis meetings in Liverpool. The Finance and Strategy Committee, he said, had a built-in Labour majority of seven. The absence of one or two councillors was not then that significant. Substitutions, he said, were allowed, so voting would not be affected.

He told them: "So the question before us as to whether we should adjourn to accommodate Mr Hatton at a later date, is only capable of one answer. The answer is no."

The Militant Young Socialist, Frances Curran didn't let Kinnock off the hook without giving him some stick. Would he be happy, she suggested, if it came down to making decisions about redundancies, cuts or the spending of £27 million, to have someone else standing in for him? What's more, she said, the letter from my solicitors made it plain that I was happy to take part in meetings right up to July 20th.

Finally they went to a vote. What a farce. As Dennis Skinner said, the cards had all been marked. Six for the adjournment, twelve against, was the vote, and they set out exactly as Kinnock had planned, to convict me in my absence.

I was charged with membership of Militant Tendency, and breach of party rules and standing orders. The charges had been set out in a letter on April 18th. Larry Whitty was cast as Witch-finder General.

Whitty read the charge that I was ineligible for membership of the Labour Party, because I was a member of Militant Tendency, a political organisation with its own programme, principles, policy and distinctive and separate propaganda which was ineligible for affiliation to the party.

My solicitors had requested that witnesses should be present, and the NEC had before it letters from Garston MP Eddie Loyden, "Leader" John Hamilton, Labour Whip Jimmy Parry and Chairman Hugh Dalton. The letters were in support of Tony Mulhearn, but we wanted the four of them to appear as witnesses for me too. Predictably, Whitty was opposed to them appearing.

He told the NEC that it was clear I didn't deny my support for the *Militant* newspaper: the issue was not whether I was a sympathiser, but whether I was member of Militant. The evidence, he said, indicated I had a substantial involvement with Militant. He cited advertisements in *Militant* for meetings in 1985 in Blackpool, Newcastle, Newcastle-under-Lyme, Birkenhead, Glasgow, Birmingham, Wales, and London, at which I was supposed to speak.

His next piece of so-called evidence was a leaflet, in which my name was among those calling for support for the *Militant* newspaper. According to Whitty it was unlikely that someone who was not centrally involved in the organisation of Militant would have signed such a leaflet and endorsed it.

He also quoted issues of *Mersey Militant* in which my name appeared in connection with articles and interviews. I denied that I had written any of them – but Whitty said he found that difficult to accept.

Whitty also raised my alleged involvement with the Mersey Action Group, which he said I had helped set up and encourage within the black community in Liverpool, to support the appointment of Sam Bond as our principal race relations adviser. According to Whitty the group was nothing more or less than a front for Militant supporters, and was designed to counter opposition in some quarters to Sam Bond's appointment. This was in spite of the fact that in the local elections the group had fielded a candidate who had opposed Militant views and opposed the Labour Party.

Taken together, he claimed, this proved central involvement on my part in organising Militant Tendency on Merseyside. He said he had requested an undertaking that I would cease to be involved with Militant Tendency, and would not become involved in their activities in the future. In my reply I had indicated that if the NEC required an undertaking that I would not have any future financial or organisational association with Militant Tendency I would be prepared to consider it, but only if this did not automatically imply my past association.

Whitty submitted that the evidence proved my membership of Militant. At that stage he would have submitted that the moon was made of green cheese if it helped throw me out of the Party.

Eric Heffer pointed out that Derek Hatton was not alone in having spoken on Militant platforms. Members of the NEC had done the same thing! It was no crime for a member of the Labour Party to do so. Michael Foot, the ex-leader, had spoken on *Morning Star* platforms at the time when it was considered the organ of the Communist Party. Members of the party had spoken on platforms supporting a variety of newspapers including *Tribune*.

So far as the leaflet was concerned, said Eric, maybe I should not have put my name to it, but if it was such a crime then everyone whose name appeared, many of them Liverpool councillors, should appear before the NEC. If one was guilty, he said, then we all were.

Where the Mersey Action Group was concerned, he said, letters from Tony Byrne and another councillor, Tony Hood, had made it clear that the appointment of Sam Bond was a Labour group decision, and nothing to do with Derek Hatton as an individual. As for writing for *Mersey Militant*, said Eric, he had himself given interviews for left-wing newspapers, and they had then appeared under his name as though he had written them.

He hadwritten for the *Times*, the *Guardian*, the *Daily Telegraph*, the *Morning Star* and a whole list of newspapers. Did this make him an ardent supporter of their political views?

Eric told the NEC: "These charges could be applied to a lot of people in this party. Are we coming down to the point that we are really concerned with people's political positions rather than the nature of the charges?

"Are we talking about a party within a party, because if we are going into that, then that was what Nye Bevan was told. Bevan and Stafford Cripps were actually expelled because of their politics and their political positions."

Heffer spoke at length. As Derek Hatton was not present, he said, he felt it his duty to stand up and speak for me. That did not mean to say he agreed with everything I said. That was irrelevant. The witnesses were not present, their evidence had been brushed aside, and yet the likes of John Hamilton, and Hugh Dalton, who had both offered to give evidence, were stalwarts who were the real Labour Party and had been from the day anyone could remember.

Instead, though, they were prepared to listen to the evidence of ex-Maoists, members of the International Marxist Group – let alone members of the Labour Party. "If Hatton is responsible then all the members of the Labour group are responsible," said Eric. "They should either all be here or none of them should be here.

"On the second charge that there were irregularities in the conduct of the Party on Merseyside you cannot say one person is more responsible than another. If you do, what you are really saying is that the people in the Liverpool Labour Party are a bunch of cretins who are afraid to speak up and act independently and are not prepared to make a stand on an issue.

"That is a damned insult to the people of Liverpool, and the members of our Party in Liverpool. If Hatton is guilty in the same way we said Tony Mulhearn was guilty, then they are all guilty, and I don't think you can differentiate.

"You are picking out a few individuals because of their basic political positions. I ask this executive to at last wake up to what's happening and decide we have had enough of this. Let's stop it now."

Tony Benn spoke up too, making comments he would never air publicly. "Hatton is to be expelled because Neil Kinnock decided to attack him at the Labour Party conference, and ever since then it has been a question of a vote of confidence in the leader of the Party.

"That is the reason in my opinion, and it is one which is very widely shared. You can buy rhapsodic praise from the Tory press if you attack the Left of the Labour Party. It has been done by other leaders but never ever in my life, as sharply as was done by the leader at the conference. From that day to this Hatton's fate has been sealed. When David Blunkett moved the inquiry into the Liverpool Party in my opinion he knew it would have the effect of expelling Hatton." Blunkett didn't like that! But Benn stuck to his guns. That was his honest opinion, he said, and he was sticking to it.

He continued: "I don't think for a moment that any argument which I put forward will influence the executive. That isn't the reason I'm making it. I believe the arguments have to be set out because I think our procedures have been in breach of natural justice, and in breach of fair play as would be understood by any ordinary member of the Party.

"No witnesses, no legal representation, and improper questioning. The methods used have been guilt by association, but to write in a newspaper, to attend a meeting publicly or privately to be a member of a group which includes people who are not members of the Labour Party has been true of every single member of this National Executive.

"I believe the public and the Party are beginning to understand that the real motive is fear: fear of the ideas put forward, an intense dislike of being criticised, and fear that if we don't crush this group the media will be more hostile to us in the election.

"I believe that to use a vote of confidence is to misuse democracy, because the choice has been put: are you for Kinnock or Militant? The answer is I want Neil to be prime minister of the country, but I do not see why that desire should leave me, and others, in the position of being anti-Militant.

"The effect of this campaign, which has gone on now for nine months, and will continue to conference and beyond, is to tell the public that there is a cancer within the Labour Party and that charge is one that will stick.

"However many people you expel there is always somebody else we won't have expelled. I believe this is a political and not a disciplinary or constitutional question. I think it brings the party into disrepute, because, for one thing, in order to pursue these charges we are having to behave in exactly the way we claim that Militant or Stalinists behave. Namely to force our way to the decision we want without regard to the evidence."

Tony's eloquence is, on occasions, beyond compare. I could not have asked for a better advocate. As for his conclusion, I can only describe it as masterly.

"I have served in Parliament under six leaders. Attlee, Gaitskell, Wilson, Callaghan, Michael Foot and now under Neil Kinnock; I was first elected to the executive twenty-seven years ago. I have never in my life experienced such a sustained attack upon left-wing and Socialist members of the Labour Party as under the present leadership. Never.

"Gaitskell talked about Communists, fellow travellers, and bearded weirdies but he never tried to pursue – principled right-wing leader that he was – expulsions on this scale. It gives an impression quite contrary to that conveyed by the Labour Party press office. It gives an impression of weakness, panic and cowardice and that we cannot argue our case in the Party on its merits. We insist on getting them out."

Tony never said a truer word. His eloquence, his anger and his dignity were lost on Kinnock and his cohorts. They voted – and they voted to expel.

THE FINAL HOURS

I have already said that 1986 was a fateful year, and as it drew to a close time was literally running out for me. In July, a month after the decision to expel me from the Labour Party, my bosses at Knowsley Borough Council decided to expel me from my job as a community development officer. That same month I and the forty-six other rebel councillors had lost an Appeal Court hearing against our disqualification, and our only hope now lay with the appeal to the House of Lords which was due to take place in January 1987.

The annual Labour Party conference was set for September 29th, 1986 in Blackpool, and the eight of us who had been expelled for our links with Militant had the right to appeal against our expulsions. We were to be item number one on the agenda. What's more our appeals were to be heard behind closed doors in secret session. It was Star Chamber all over again!

On the day, one of the eight, Terry Harrison, one of the founders of Militant back in the 1960s, was too ill to attend. That left myself, Tony Mulhearn and Ian Lowes, to face the music along with the four others. There was Richard Venton, Militant's organiser on Merseyside; his girlfriend Cheryl Varley who was a leading Labour Party Young Socialist; Josie Aitman, a member of the suspended District Labour Party Executive; and her husband Tony, a former shop steward and regular contributor to the *Militant* newspaper.

None of us had any illusions about the outcome. A campaign by Kinnock and the trade union leaders to ensure that our expulsions were ratified by conference had been going on for months, and the block votes of the unions had already been lined up against us. They wanted to see Thatcher out of Downing Street and to do that were giving Neil Kinnock an open ticket. If he said Hatton and the rest must go, then go we must.

We were herded into an anteroom off the main conference hall of the Winter Gardens in Blackpool. It was ironic that for our execution we should be lined up on the scaffold in the very place where only two years before we had been the conquering heroes who had wrung more money for the council out of Patrick Jenkin. Now the heroes were told that they had five minutes, individually in alphabetical order, to speak in their defence.

It was an outrage. Among the seven of us we represented over 100 years' membership of the Labour Party. We told General Secretary Larry Whitty that we could not possibly do justice to our case in so short a time. Nobody listened. They had already decided to hear the appeals in camera because they didn't want to give us a platform on which we could publicly convince, not just the conference, but the country, of the justice of our case. So there was no way they were going to give us more time.

The conference hall was buzzing. But not with the kind of excitement we had shared with the delegates back in 1984. This time it was almost a blood lust. They were like the mob waiting at the guillotine for the tumbrels to arrive. But we were not going to give them the bloody spectacle they wanted. We refused to take the platform.

One by one as we were called it was announced that we had demanded more time, and as our final protest, would not appear before conference unless that demand was met. You could tell the mood. Our decision was greeted with boos, jeers and slow hand-clapping. Half an hour later the 1986 Labour Party Conference voted by twenty to one to back the expulsions.

Kinnock was exultant. He actually said: "I am not surprised by their behaviour. These are the people who purported to speak for the rank and file Labour Party. But when it came to it, they do not have the spine to speak for themselves."

What arrogant nonsense! There was nothing we had done in those three years which had not already been agreed in principle by Labour Party conferences over the years. The trade unions too had voted for the kind of policies that we actually put into effect. The truth was that it was Kinnock and the rest who had no spine. When the going got tough and they had to face the reality of a battle with the Government in the Liverpool campaign, they lost their nerve.

They were frightened of the support we could muster – the trade union leaders because their rank and file membership was turning against them in support of Liverpool and heading for direct conflict with the Government – the Labour Party bureaucracy because they saw a groundswell of working-class opinion which they would be unable to control if it got out of hand. Most importantly we had a Labour leader who did not want a campaign which raised in people's minds expectations that he would be expected to fulfil by providing jobs and protecting services no matter what the cost.

He also believed that the middle ground in politics in this country was going to be swayed by taking an anti-Militant stance. The Tory press even boasted that Kinnock had followed their line in expelling Militants from the party.

From the moment we were thrown out of the Labour Party

it was clear that some serious decisions would have to be taken about our role in the running of Liverpool City Council. Our appeal to the House of Lords against disqualification as councillors was still pending – so there was nothing to prevent us from continuing our work for the council. But could we stay on in the ruling Labour group?

Publicly we said that the group would refuse to accept the expulsions. Privately I realised, and so did Tony Mulhearn, that there were far-reaching political implications. Would I have to resign as deputy leader of the Labour group? Would I be thrown out of office altogether?

The Labour Party's National Executive Committee had decided to force a final showdown, to bring the Liverpool Labour group back into line. They demanded that I resign my deputy leadership, that Tony Mulhearn and I should resign our committee chairmanships – along with Councillor Felicity Dowling whose expulsion was still pending – and that the Labour group should disown us.

Larry Whitty, and another of Kinnock's aides, Joyce Gould, summoned a meeting of the Labour group. The intention was that other Labour councillors would be appointed to take our places.

I heard from Tony Byrne that he had received a letter from Whitty, telling him that unless he was prepared to renounce me and the positions that I held, he would face disciplinary action by the Labour Party.

The lobby within the group which for years had campaigned for the sacking of the leader – John Hamilton – now grew. Opinions about John had ranged from those who thought that he was a nice old man who at best was ignorant of what was going on, to the feeling that he was a mischievous old man who got in the way of things happening. But up to that time the argument had been carried by those who said that to depose him would be seen as a personal not a political assassination. Sacking him, they insisted, would only damage our cause.

Now, with the Whitty meeting imminent, what had been seen as equivocation on John's part was perceived as political treachery. He had begun publicly to denounce me and others, after going along with us as leader throughout the three years. Nevertheless before the Whitty meeting we hit on a strategy. At a get-together of the broad Left – not only Militants but also those Labour councillors who still supported Tony Mulhearn and me – we decided that John Hamilton would be left in place as leader of the group, but we would not fill the deputy leader's place which I would vacate. Instead, even though I had resigned I would still be deputy leader of the council, which was not a Labour Party appointment. That was the stance we decided to take.

Matters, however, took a dramatic turn, and once more, by their clumsy ineptitude, the NEC found themselves on the spot. Larry Whitty sent out letters to each member of the Labour group due to attend the meeting on Thursday, November 20th, 1986, warning them that unless they sent back written confirmation that they were prepared to abide totally by the constitution and disassociate themselves from those of us who had been expelled, they would not be allowed to attend the meeting.

It was like a red rag to a bull. A minority – on the right wing and the soft Left – deserted, among them John Hamilton, who had no hesitation in denouncing me and what I stood for. The rest signed identical letters and went into the meeting. But Whitty's tactics were about to backfire on him. The group went in reminding themselves that the plan was to leave Hamilton in place as leader, to elect Tony Byrne as chairman and to leave the deputy leadership vacant.

But Whitty vetoed the move. There would not, he said, be separate votes for chairman and leader. The two positions were synonymous. The response was one of fury, almost a reaction that two could play at that game. Play it they did – nominating Tony Byrne as the leader. People pleaded with Whitty to change his mind, realising what was about to happen, but so inept was he that he let the motion go to a vote.

By a clear majority Tony Byrne was elected leader. Larry Whitty, by his dogmatic attitude, had allowed to happen something which even the hard Left had resisted all those years. John Hamilton, the tired little old man who had clung onto power no matter what, had finally been ditched. When I heard, my initial reaction was to stop laughing long enough to find out what had really gone on. I couldn't believe it. The NEC had shot themselves in the foot again. Tony Byrne was the leader, Hamilton was out, and none of it had been part of our plan. I could just imagine Larry Whitty on the telephone to Neil Kinnock trying to explain how they had managed to do it. Joyce Gould was actually overheard saying to Whitty: "We've made a right balls of this."

In the cold light of day next morning I knew it would backfire on us as well, and so it did for a time. I received countless calls from political friends, businessmen, even ordinary folk in the street. All of them were delighted that I was still working in the background and that Tony Byrne was in power, but they all questioned the sacking of Hamilton. I thought it was a reaction which might build, but over the next few days it died, and Hamilton himself helped kill it off.

The press and the public were treated to the sad spectacle of a toppled leader trying to drum up support, and denying what had been a democratic vote. He had gone along with the democracy which threw us out and told him to denounce us. Now he wanted his bread buttered on both sides, and would not accept that Tony Byrne was the democratically elected leader. It was a two-faced performance which won him no friends and cost him what sympathy there had been.

I knew, though, which way the tide was running now. If Tony Byrne continued to support me, he himself would be expelled. I had to ask myself whether it was worth sacrificing the whole structure just to defend those who had been expelled – especially as we knew full well that even without us in positions of power our policies could still continue. Kinnock wanted Derek Hatton. He would be pleased with that – why give him anything else?

By Sunday night November 23rd, 1986 I had made up my mind. I would have to go.

Monday was a difficult day. I spoke to my own staff in the council offices, who were fiercely loyal and wanted me to stand and fight. The pressure though from members of the Labour group became intense as the day progressed and word got round that I had decided to resign. They argued that they didn't want to be a part of a Labour Party which did not include us, and that as we had all gone into the battle together we should end it together.

Other people however understood the inevitability of it all, no one more so than Peter Taaffe at Militant headquarters in London. I rang him and gave him my decision. Peter was in no doubt that it was the right one. For the sake of the Labour and trade union movement, and for the sake of Socialism in the future, he said, it was important that the Labour Party was not denuded of good quality Lefts, the likes of Tony Byrne, and my own Militant colleague, Paul Astbury, who was eventually to follow me into the deputy leader's position. The important thing was that they stay and continue the fight for Socialism within the party.

As a friend for many years he was clearly sorry to see the three of us losing our positions on the council, but I remember him saying to me: "Look Derek, we have a long way to go within the Labour Party. The party will exist until we achieve Socialism and the trade union movement is not going to go away either. We are the lifeblood of the party. Our job is to build up support for the ideas of genuine Socialism within the party. We must ensure that the likes of Kinnock are not given a free hand to take this party to the Right. While the sacrifice of yourself, Felicity Dowling and Tony Mulhearn, is a great sacrifice to have to make, we must acknowledge it is better than having to sacrifice others as well."

It was, and is true, of course, that the right wing of the NEC was acting in such a manner, and Kinnock had now made the assault on Militant such a personal one, that they would have sacrificed the whole of the Labour group in Liverpool if need be just to make their point. It was Peter's analysis of the situation which dispelled any doubts I might have had, and reaffirmed in my mind the correctness of my decision.

Others argued on a more personal level, pointing out that human nature being what it is, if I stayed and dragged others down with me I would eventually be blamed for that. Whereas if I was seen to go with dignity that would be a tribute. That night, at the meeting of the broad Left group I announced my decision. Tony Mulhearn and Felicity Dowling took the same stand. We spelt out our arguments, but there were still those who insisted on having their dissent recorded. The decision was made though. I would resign next day.

The evening of November 24th, 1986 was one I shall always remember. I had not told Shirley of my decision on the Sunday. I hadn't felt like talking to anyone about it. Sometimes there are moments when I just have to sit and work these things out alone. I knew anyway that she would have reacted with absolute loyalty, and she would have been concerned about the effect it would have on me. Now I told her. She understood completely and accepted as I did that it was inevitable.

Next I rang Mam and Dad. Dad was quite predictable, threatening to "wring that Kinnock's neck if I get hold of him". Mam was simply upset. She wanted to know every detail of what had happened during the day, but then, in the practical way that she has, she was more concerned about what the future held: what I would do, where I would work. At that stage it was the kind of objectivity I needed.

Normally, no matter what the problems of the day, I usually fall asleep without any trouble. That night I didn't. I don't think I was upset, but my mind was churning. It was such an important decision that no matter what, I was bound to go on questioning it. I can think of no one who, faced with the end of a whole part of their life, would not have reacted as I did. That three and a half years had made a tremendous impact on me as an individual.

Over breakfast next day the children all had questions to ask. Would I still be a councillor? What was I going to do now? What would my new job be? We talked for a while, then I left for the council offices and the press conference which was to mark the end of an era for me.

I have attended, and held sway, at more news conferences than most people, but this one felt different from the moment I walked in. There were cameras crammed into every corner of the room. There was no way that I was going in with my chin down, so I adopted my usual jokey, bubbly approach, and bounced into the room as I always have. The strange thing was that some of the journalists there seemed almost saddened by the occasion. I was bouncing. They were not.

I seldom write speeches in advance. Sometimes I'll jot down a few key words, but on this occasion I didn't need those. I had been thinking all night what I would say, and they were summed up in the three words which became the headlines that evening: sad, bitter and proud. Sad that after all we had gone through I was leaving when there was so much more to do. Bitter towards the right-wing leadership of the Labour Party, who, in splitting the Labour group, had managed to do something which even the courts and the Tory press had been unable to achieve. Proud of our achievements in the city, and the way we had over those years kept the Labour group united.

It was a speech which was much more personal than political. Normally when confronted with politicians like Thatcher or commentators like Robin Day I can rant, rave and battle with the best of them. But this was different.

I think that even those journalists who had become my political enemies understood what I was trying to say, and that was reflected in the coverage that night and next day. Papers which normally would not have been able to find a good word to say about me at least managed to convey the impression that I had tried to bow out with dignity.

In January 1987 the House of Lords began hearing the final appeal by myself and the other forty-six "rebel" councillors against the surcharges and disqualification. We were now face to face with the prospect of political and personal bankruptcy.

The financial implications were enormous. The legal costs alone for the appeal were crippling, and we had been forced to hold collections, and pull in donations and loans from the trade union movement to pay our legal bills. At one stage it was estimated that, with the surcharge, they could amount to more than a £250,000.

So it was quite a relief, when, having changed our solicitors, most of us were granted legal aid for the Lords appeal. I suspect that the Law Society finally gave way because they recognised that publicly it might seem strange that for such an important issue we should be denied the justice we sought for lack of money, whether people agreed with our cause or not.

I went down to the first day's hearing of our appeal to the House of Lords. I stayed for an hour, then walked out. It was like watching paint dry: five men without a wig or a gown among them, sitting there like a committee analysing every dot and comma in the arguments. It was astonishing to think that no matter what the Government said they were the law of the land on issues like this. Tony Byrne on the other hand was fascinated by the proceedings, and sat through them hour after hour.

Judgement Day was Thursday, March 12th, 1987. About half the councillors decided they would be there, at the Lords, to hear the verdict. I decided though that there was only one place to see the end of this battle, in the Town Hall in Liverpool where the fight had begun.

When the phone call came from London the verdict was no surprise. The five law lords had unanimously thrown out our appeal. At two o'clock that afternoon, as they handed down their verdict, all forty-seven of us were disqualified from office for five years, and ordered to pay surcharges and costs totalling £333,000.

Five law lords had sat in judgement over councillors who had been democratically elected, and were able to throw democracy out of the window. Whatever people might think of Derek Hatton, Tony Byrne, Tony Mulhearn and the rest we had been elected by the people, and it was up to them to remove us in the same way if they didn't want us. No matter what their judgement, if I had the opportunity to go back over that three and a half years I would have done the same again.

In many ways that Thursday was not the worst day. It was the previous day that I really found the most difficult. I knew what was coming, and spent the time clearing my desk, and my papers, and saying my goodbyes to people in the council offices. I had a long discussion with Tony Byrne in the office where we had made so many plans and nurtured so many dreams. Now we were discussing the end of an era. We knew we would never again have a discussion in that office, and suddenly I felt very flat. I suppose it was like waiting for someone to die: once they were dead although the tears were there you could get on with arranging the funeral and trying to build for the future.

But whatever my feelings, and those of people around me, it was a great comfort at that stage to know that in the background, supporting whatever I did, was Shirley.

'I have been asked if I could have stood in Derek's place once he was thrown out of office. The answer is no. Not with the commitment that he gave which was total. He and the rest have been placed on a pedestal and labelled as rebels simply because they set out to keep the promises they made when they come to power.

When his expulsion from the Labour Party and his disqualification from office became a possibility, we were faced with the reality that our whole life, our finances and our home could be on the line. Derek never wavered, neither did I. When you have committed yourself so totally to an ideal, and become so involved, you have to see it through to the end, no matter what that may be. I never believed we would lose everything, because I'm just not the kind of person who could dwell on that sort of possibility.

I don't feel any bitterness, just anger that Derek and the rest have been betrayed by the Party to which some of them have given all their lives. They were all devastated by it. To Derek it was his way of life. Suddenly to be told that it's finished doesn't seem real. Derek was shattered, but more than anything he was saddened. Saddened that people like Neil Kinnock, who had a duty to do so, had not been to Liverpool and spent time seeing the problems for themselves and discussing them with the Labour group. Maybe he might never have agreed with their point of view, but at least he would have come out of it with honour.

But Neil Kinnock must realise now that he won't stop the groundswell which Derek and the rest began. You can expel someone from the party, and throw them out of the council. What you cannot do is prevent them thinking and getting together with those who think as they do. Liverpool is still there. So are its problems, and Derek will always want to be a part of the fight against those problems.

Looking to the future, life is changing for all of us, and I view that with mixed feelings. Derek has come to a point where changes have been forced, and he has a lot of decisions to make, but he is more relaxed now than he has ever been. We have more time to enjoy each other's company, and as the children grow older I can take the opportunity to go with him when he travels around the country.

Obviously I enjoy that, and with Derek there's never a dull moment. When he was invited to appear on the Wogan show after being thrown out of office I went too, and we travelled down by train. It was shortly after the heavy snows, and I was gazing out of the window at the countryside, which was simply beautiful.

Derek though had his head stuck in a copy of The Merchant of Venice. He was convinced that Wogan might pick up on the fact that he had been in the play while he was at school, and wanted to be ready to quote some of the lines over again. It was hilarious. The man sitting opposite us must have thought we were quite mad, because Derek suddenly took his nose out of the book, passed it across to me, and said: "Test me." Then he set about delivering some of Shylock's lines, giving it every ounce of projection and dramatic effect he could, complete with an accent!

Then of course there have been numerous invitations for him to appear as a personality in his own right at dinners, debates, and even in films and at fashion shows. None of that means that he has lost any of his commitment to Liverpool and the things he has tried to do for the city.

When he comes home the kids bounce round him, and fight to be the one who sits next to him, but the phone still goes, the doorbell still rings, and there are still people asking if he can help with their problems. What's more you have to spare that time, and I don't begrudge it. Derek is not the sort of person to do anything by halves. He went into politics in Liverpool to fight for everything, and just because they have thrown him out doesn't make him any the less concerned about his own city.

I don't think too hard about the years ahead – one day at a time is very much my philosophy. We are both Capricorns, but different in many ways. He has so much energy and never tires, and where politics is concerned he gives everything he has.

Derek lost his job. He lost his position. He was thrown out of the Labour Party to which he had given so much. But no matter what has happened, and no matter what people say about us in the rumour and gossip which is spread, we have a smashing marriage. We are mates, we are best friends, we are part of each other.

EPILOGUE

Looking back over those three and a half years in office in Liverpool I still feel sadness and pride: sadness because I will miss playing the part that I did in making the decisions which would change people's lives, and pride that there will never again be a group of Labour councillors who will be able to stand firm in the way we did, no matter what splits eventually developed.

As for Neil Kinnock, and the rest of the Labour Party leadership, their actions only serve to underline my belief that until they are removed, and the Party moves back to its proper place on the true Left of British politics, we shall not see a Labour Government in power.

The defeat in the General Election of 1987 is proof, if ever it was needed, that Kinnock's campaign to root out Militant did not enhance Labour's image, but damaged it. He saw us as an electoral liability, but it is Kinnock himself who must shoulder responsibility for an election disaster of that magnitude.

In my assessment, Neil Kinnock will go down in history as the worst Labour leader we've ever had. He would move to the Right far faster in government than Ramsay McDonald did. I have no doubt about that. In the wake of the election defeat his attempts to create a new brand of "yuppie" Socialism make that abundantly clear.

In my opinion the tragedy is that that he does not have the sense to combine his forces against Thatcher. Instead he is divisive. If you take Harold Wilson as a comparison, even though he was at odds with the Left, he took the line that while in Opposition he would support every campaign against the Heath Government, no matter from which quarter the attack came.

The other thing that can be said about Wilson, and about Jim Callaghan, is that they had experience. For all their right-wing politics, with which I disagreed, they had political wisdom. That is a quality in which Neil Kinnock is sadly lacking.

My earliest recollections of him are at Labour Party conferences, where year after year he took the collections at Tribune rallies. It is ironic that the man who now rails against groups within the party should have been so much a part of Tribune, which in its early days was regarded with great distrust by the leadership. Kinnock was good at collecting money. He always had a ready line in wit and cracking jokes. Neil Kinnock's problems began when he stopped joking and started trying to be serious.

My bitterness against him is not personal, but political. I think he is destroying the Labour Party, and has redefined Socialism. It is a measure of his ineptitude that even after expelling us, in a purge which was supposed to cleanse and purify the party, he still couldn't manage to beat Thatcher at a time of record unemployment.

In Liverpool, where Labour has not lost an election battle from 1983 onwards, Militant has proved its worth. But Kinnock chose to chop off those good arms of the Party, leaving it to stand on unsteady legs, supported by those who were prepared to listen to the editorials of the Tory press. They wanted to try and attract the SDP and Alliance vote, and somehow to pretend that the Labour Party could be more Conservative than the Conservatives.

Kinnock's tactical errors were, in my view, blunders which could do nothing but damage. As he moved more and more to the Right, he became increasingly unpopular with the activists within his own party who wanted to see radical changes under true Socialism. At the same time he could not win the moderate middle-class ground he so desperately wooed, because no one trusts a politician who can cut his policies to pander to prevailing public opinion.

He would not support the miners, he would not support the battle in Liverpool, he would not support the struggles at Wapping. Labour Party leaders before him have always, in Opposition, realised the need to support the struggles of the working class no matter on which front they were being fought. The Labour leadership under Kinnock, to its eternal disgrace, chose not to get involved in campaigns like those. They adopted a stance which seemed to say that they were taking the side of the employers, and not the trade unions. Ultimately it led to the view that if Britain was to be governed by a Tory Party, it might as well be a Party which is truly Conservative rather than a Labour Party which is trying to ape it.

It was clear to me during the General Election campaign – when in spite of all that had happened I did go out canvassing for Labour on the doorstep – that this was a view held by many people. I found it quite common for people to ask why they should vote for Labour, when all the Party had done was help destroy the very council the people of Liverpool had voted into power. You found yourself trying to persuade people to vote Labour in spite of Kinnock and not because of him.

Since the election defeat Kinnock still has not learned his lesson. The expulsions have continued – fellow Liverpool councillor Felicity Dowling whose case was adjourned in 1986 was thrown out the following year – and he is still alienating those on the Left of the party. What is more it seems to me now that there is a great body of Labour Party supporters which, though desperate to get rid of Thatcher, is scared of challenging Kinnock, and has begun to believe his propaganda that a move to the Left will harm their cause.

It will be some time, in my view, before they realise that Kinnock has to be taken on before they will ever have the chance of winning an election. It is now highly unlikely that Kinnock will ever become prime minister, and I think it will be a long time before the Labour Party becomes a party of power again. Thatcher is still demonstrating that she is an effective leader. She stands up as she did after the election victory and says what she means – and believes it. Kinnock stands up and seems to say he's not sure what he believes or we believe – so let us all go away and think about it, then come back and think about it again.

Now Kinnock finds it convenient to attack the activities of the loony London left. It is certainly true that gay liberation, chairpeople as opposed to chairmen, and token black mayors won't be the things which win us support from workers be they black or white. That is why he tried to lump us in with them, and that is where he makes a fundamental mistake.

He must understand people's aspirations and expectations under a Labour Government. They will want pay rises, factories and jobs, homes and hospitals. They won't expect the money to come from the individual by way of major tax increases, and Kinnock, given his policy of appeasement towards them, won't take it from the major international and multi-national companies as he should. If he did so, it would be to concede some of what we say in Militant. He will find himself attacked on all sides, and if there is one thing Kinnock cannot face it is conflict with the likes of the Derek Hattons of this world. It appears to me that he is a man who insists on being number one, and unchallenged, he is a very apolitical person, a very apolitical leader, a careerist.

His present paranoia about Militant stems from the fact that here in Liverpool we proved that you can do all the things he said were impossible. For instance, he labelled us a Labour Party vote-loser. In fact the opposite is true. We have never lost a local election in Liverpool since 1983. In fact in the 1983 General Election the only Tory marginal in the country won by Labour was in Broadgreen, where Terry Fields, a declared Militant supporter, was elected. If that result had been reflected across the country we would have had a 100-seat Labour majority. By comparison, in Knowsley North and in Newcastle, Kinnock has shown by trying to purge Militant, and imposing his own right-wing candidates, he can halve a Labour majority in mid-term, a time when we should be romping home in by-elections against the Tories and the Alliance.

So if Kinnock claims we are an electoral liability, with a few more liabilities like us we should be home and dry at the next election.

What we had in Liverpool was the best possible example of how Labour can win elections. That is not an argument about the politics of Liverpool, but a simple fact. We actually won support, and the figures proved it.

So, what of the future, for me, for Militant and for the Labour Party?

It's true to say that I may have been thrown out of office, and out of the Party, but I've hardly been thrown out of the public gaze. Having lost my job with Knowsley Council, I still had to earn a living. My biggest asset was my mouth – and my knowledge of the way that local government works. I decided to combine the two, and set up my own company, Settleside Ltd, to act as a public and industrial relations consultant. Local authority bureaucracy often moves in a painfully slow and ponderous manner. It's a labyrinth through which companies and businessmen have to find their way when they are planning anything, from new buildings to expansion of existing operations. Often they can waste valuable months ploughing through the red tape put in their way by what I used to call the municipal mafia. I argued that there was a ready market for someone like

171

myself who could offer his expertise in guiding them through that maze.

It was that decision which put me right back in the headlines again. The tabloid press couldn't wait to start knocking me once more.

This time they decided I was a "closet capitalist", and of course, they started trotting out all the old, old stories about my smart suits, my so-called jet-set lifestyle and the women with whom I was seen. Because I was still in demand to appear as a celebrity on television programmes, and at anything from a fashion show to a VIP party, I was good material for the gossip columns too.

You just can't win with the press. I was criticised when I was dressing too smartly. I was criticised when I was being too left-wing politically. Now I was being criticised for running a business, making a living and generally surviving. They would have loved to see me on the dole in sackcloth and ashes.

I make no apologies for it all. I see no conflict between the way I live and the political beliefs that I hold. I still know that the only way in which the Labour Party is going to be a strong force in British politics is if Militant is in its leadership.

I still financially support Militant – and always will. It is very much a part of the Labour Party, no matter what the constitution says. Its ideas are rooted within the Party both nationally and locally. Militant supporters will never argue that they should be outside. They must work from within. It is a case of ensuring change from within. There are all too many stupid revolutionary groups on the fringes who have achieved nothing, and never will. But where Militant is concerned, whether the Labour Party recognises us or not, there are thousand upon thousand Militants within, and their number is growing daily. It would be wrong now to see a mass exodus, and hand Kinnock the chance or excuse to root more of them out.

What Militant says now is little different from the things said by Keir Hardie when he founded the Labour Party. The whole concept of taking control of the means of production, the heights of the economy, is, for example, embodied in Clause Four of the Labour Party's constitution. Whilst many members of the Parliamentary Labour Party, and the NEC, would like to see it removed they have not succeeded yet. Even if they took away the words they could not remove the deep-rooted conviction among the rank and file that those principles are enshrined in tablets of stone.

So Militant is a force within the Party which can never be ignored. Sadly though, but for one major blunder, I believe Militant would be even stronger now. They knuckled under to Kinnock when in 1986, at the beginning of the witch-hunt, the National Executive suspended the Liverpool District Labour Party.

It is one of the issues on which to this day I believe that Peter Taaffe and the rest of Militant were wrong.

We accepted the decision, albeit under protest, with Peter Taaffe, Tony Mulhearn, and many other Militants, including those on the editorial board, arguing that if we did not go along with suspension, then many other members of the Party, both Militant and those on the good Left, would also face expulsion. To stand firm and defy the NEC over suspension would, it was argued, be attempting to find a short-term solution to a long-term problem.

Historically, Militant will always argue in favour of the long-term strategy, and had said, on that occasion, that Militant supporters should not stand accused of going against the Labour Party constitution. The theory was that while eight or nine of us might be thrown out, the District Labour Party would at some stage be revived, and the Militants left inside would be there to take over.

Much better, it was claimed, that people like Tony Mulhearn and I should be sacrificed rather than expose others to the same risks. To this day I still think it was the biggest mistake we ever made, and I believe history has proved me right.

The District Labour Party was the Militant power base, its anchor. It had taken years to build our position there, yet we handed it over without a whimper. I am certain that Neil

Kinnock could not believe his luck when we accepted what was happening.

Had we challenged the suspension it would certainly, to a degree, have isolated us, but it would also have isolated the whole of the party in Liverpool. Kinnock would have been forced to expel every last member of the Labour group, including the likes of John Hamilton. We would still have had the forum to win our arguments through debate and discussion as we had over the years. Instead we gave that platform away. As a result, much of our previous influence and support was lost.

Who knows what is in store for Derek Hatton? I have accepted the fact that I will no longer be a councillor, and that no matter how great my interest I won't carry the same political clout. One thing which won't change is my belief that the people of Liverpool deserve a better deal, and in every way I can I will still be battling and fighting for the city. Nothing that Neil Kinnock and the rest of the Labour rump can do will change that.

Though I am banned from holding council office for five years I could stand for Parliament. I was asked on three occasions to put myself forward as a Parliamentary candidate, but always felt that I had more important things to do in Liverpool. I still don't see myself in that role. Anyway, as Tony Benn once said to me, the only person who ever went into Parliament with honourable intent was Guy Fawkes.

A chapter of my life has ended. A chapter in the battle for Socialism is over. But you can be certain of one thing: more chapters are yet to be written, and I have every intention of ensuring that the name of Derek Hatton is in them.